TAP
NOTES

A STEP BY STEP GUIDE TO TEACHING TAP CHILDREN'S EDITION

CONTENTS

INTRODUCTION

I started this manual more than twenty-five years ago, and until recently it was merely a ten-page guide for my teachers. I've always believed it could be expanded to serve as a resource for others, and I'm grateful for the inspiration I've felt from my students, teachers, colleagues and supporters to develop it into a tap-teaching manual. I'm very proud to be sharing *Thelma's Tap Notes* with you.

The motivation to document my approach to tap instruction stems from my commitment to education. Before opening the Dance Inn in 1983, I was a special education teacher in Boston for eight years. Knowing that confidence in basic skills would provide the foundation for future development, I learned to break down the simplest of academic tasks so that my students could experience success. When I founded my studio, I approached dance education with a similar objective: how could I best train my students? I found that ballet and jazz had many teaching models to guide dance educators, but tap had few or none. While valuing the oral tradition of passing down tap steps, I wanted a more concrete method that would systematically teach students the skills for strong technique and articulate footwork. After more than thirty years in the classroom, teaching all levels of dancers, I believe the following principles are at the core of my philosophy:

- **Release** is the action of shifting weight fully so that dancers always have a foot, toe or heel in a position of readiness.
- **Relaxation** in the ankles, knees and hips allows dancers to drop into the floor, resulting in efficient and articulate percussive action.
- **Rhythmic progressions** challenge the dancer to proceed musically, mastering new skills in quarter-note time before dancing in eighth notes, triplets or sixteenth notes.
- **Full-bodied rhythm-making™** engages the whole body in learning and performing, using the voice, head and hands to reinforce clear rhythms.

I know there may be areas of my approach with which some teachers will disagree. Regardless of whether you follow the syllabus as suggested, the Combos, Choreography and Series will certainly add flavor and variety to any existing program. I hope you enjoy this manual, and that it inspires you and your students to love your tap classes!

HOW TO USE THE MANUAL

Thelma's Tap Notes is divided into two main sections. Because the approach is cumulative, there are many important notes discussed in the early sections that correlate to success with later skills. I suggest you read through all the levels and apply the recommendations that are most appropriate for your students.

About the Levels:

My school is a traditional dance studio that offers combo (Tap-Jazz-Ballet) classes for children ages 6–12, progressing from Level I to Level V. Some children will complete five levels in five years. Others will progress more quickly or will take longer. Although the notes are geared specifically to this age group, the lessons can be easily adjusted to work with all ages. The recommended Class Outline can certainly be adapted to suit your studio's schedule. The lessons and goals for each level are based on a 32-week session with the following tap time:

Level/Combo I (ages 6–7) 30 minutes tap per week
Level/Combo II (ages 7–8) 35 minutes tap per week
Level/Combo III, IV, V (ages 8–12) 45 minutes tap per week

Why I wait until 1st grade (6 yrs.) to have my students wear tap shoes:

During the preschool years, I introduce ideas like "tapping the ball of the foot," but I don't have them wear tap shoes. Instead I focus on developing gross motor skills like skipping, leaping, chassé-ing, galloping, marching, hopping and walking on the balls of the feet. Simple footwork with heel digs, toe digs and ball taps is used in choreography patterns. We work a lot with musical instruments and rhythm activities that reinforce quarter-note timing and identifying the "1," and we strengthen their right-left directionality. Shifting weight, releasing to a ready position and dancing with joy are important objectives. With a strong foundation in musicality and movement, when six-year-olds start tapping, they immediately experience success and are ready for the challenge of coordinating the two taps!

Part One includes the following information for each of five teaching levels for children ages 6–12:
*   ✻ Overview - specific technical and skill development goals for the dancer
*   ✻ Musical Rhythms - music-theory goals and rhythms for Games, Improvisation and Choreography
*   ✻ Class Outline - step-by-step guide to the weekly lesson, with **Music Recommendations**
*   ✻ The Next Step - new skills and when and how to teach them
*   ✻ Combos - combining skills in challenging and fun combos
*   ✻ Choreography - a complete dance routine for performance
*   ✻ Improvisation Activities - ideas for improvising

Part Two includes exercises and drills based on a series of progressively challenging rhythms to promote sequential progress in the major areas of tap education listed below. As you'll note, some series are not introduced until dancers are in later levels.
*   ✻ Rudiment Series - Levels I–V - from simple toe-heel patterns to traditional Condos Rudiments
*   ✻ Double Heel Series - Levels II–V - cramp rolls, press cramp rolls and more
*   ✻ Shuffle Series - Levels I–V - from a single brush and spank to swinging shuffles with hops, leaps, ball changes and more
*   ✻ Slap and Flap Series - Levels II–V - how and when to teach slaps and flaps
*   ✻ Paddle and Roll Series - Levels IV–V - exercises to reinforce relaxation and articulation in paddle and roll combos

4

* Spank Series - Levels IV–V - exercises to promote good technique in all patterns using the back brush, such as drawbacks, cross-over steps and time steps
* Time Step Series - Levels IV–V - short exercises that lead to clarity and precision in single, double and triple time steps, as well as half and full breaks

Throughout Parts One and Two, the reader will also find:
* Classic tap steps indicated with a * and, when first introduced, highlighted in a box
* Teaching Tips
* Additional "Thelma's Notes" with personal thoughts
* Vocalization cues ◌

An Addendum provides brief biographies of tap teachers and performers I have worked with or who have influenced me. A Glossary provides more information about important tap steps. In addition, a Timeline of Tap History is provided for teachers to help them share the rich heritage of this uniquely American dance form.

Reading the Notes:
* Read the rhythm line - "1 2&3 4" - rhythmically and out loud
* Read the words of the "step" in the rhythm shown
* Determine weight shifts by the Right (R) and Left (L) designations

Many teachers have their own system of recording tap steps. I have tried to keep the presentation of combinations and exercise patterns as simple and understandable as possible. Phrases are often shown in two bars, or eight counts with a REPEAT or REVERSE indicated. To "read" the notes, I suggest you first read the top line of numerical notes in the correct rhythm. Silent notes are indicated with parentheses ( ). In eighth-note triplets I use the letter "a" (pronounced "uh") to represent the third eighth note, as in "1 & a." Once you have the rhythm, say the second line, which indicates the movement. Abbreviations are shown in The Next Step section as well as in the Glossary. Try to read the steps in the right rhythm. The third line indicates the foot that is used - R(ight) or L(eft). In some cases I use an "X" to indicate a crossed foot, but I've left some of the expression of the movement up to the teacher. For example, LXBR means the left foot crosses back of the right.

Lesson Plans:
A sample lesson plan is available at the end of the book to assist teachers with using the manual. Included are three blank sample pages, one for Level I, one for Levels II and III, and one for Levels IV and V. These three blank lesson plans are organized around the different Series taught at these levels. The category of Tap Fun is included to help in planning improvisational or musical rhythm activities. Also, consider sharing video footage and story books for special Tap Fun experiences for your students.

a1 & a2

A Note About Full-Body Rhythm-Making™:

As a student of Jump Rhythm Technique®, created by Billy Siegenfeld, I always encourage my dancers to use their voices, heads and hands throughout the lesson. The voice is particularly helpful in learning the rhythm. With a rhythm-first approach, dancers "say" or "scat" the steps/counts, or express the rhythm with their hands before actually doing the footwork. Saying the steps helps dancers to learn the vocabulary; you'll notice several places where I suggest a fun rhyme to reinforce a rhythm. Likewise, the hands and head can be very expressive in exhibiting energy. Clapping the rhythm and indicating specific counts or accents with a hand or head motion will increase the overall enjoyment and clarity of the tap phrase for both the dancer and the audience. The more your students engage their whole bodies and selves in the learning process, the more dynamic and articulate they will become.

Music Recommendations:

The music suggestions are solely for illustrative purposes. No license or right to use is afforded or granted herein. Licenses to such works must be separately obtained.

When I designate a tune to be "swing," I am using it to reinforce eighth-note triplets and a swing feel. A "straight" tune has a clear duple or quadruple feel and is usually used when dancers are learning to play straight eighth notes and sixteenth notes. As dancers mature, they are able to swing to a straight tune and dance straight notes to a swing tune. Being able to identify the musical form of a song is an important skill in the development of a tap dancer.

Video Support:

Video footage and additional notes will be posted regularly on the website *www.thelmastapnotes.com*.

ACKNOWLEDGMENTS

I would not have been able to finish this project without the support of my family, including my dancing children Robin and Sebastian, who have used my methods in their own teaching and who wanted notes and instructions written down. My student Ryan P. Casey was very helpful in editing, compiling biographies and, likewise, using the techniques in his teaching. In addition, I want to thank the teachers of the Dance Teacher's Club of Boston, who participated in focus groups, and the participants in my Teacher Workshops. Their feedback has been vital to the organization and presentation of the material. Special appreciation goes to Deborah Jackson for keeping me on track with the project, to Julia Bailey for her editing prowess and to Melissa Williamson for designing a manual that demonstrates the passion behind the words. To all my friends who contributed edits and ideas: thank you! Any mistakes are mine, and I will aim to make corrections and improvements in future editions.

I'm particularly grateful to all my teachers, starting with Grace C. Bates and Joan F. O'Brien, who not only gave me the building blocks but also shared their passion, always encouraging me to be the best dancer and person I could be. Since then, many teachers have influenced my growth as a teacher and as a performer. In the order that I met them, I thank Julia Boynton, Dianne Walker, Josh Hilberman, Brenda Bufalino, Billy Siegenfeld, Jeannie Hill, Barbara Duffy and Sarah Petronio. There are many, many others, but these teachers have particularly impacted my teaching. Their passion and commitment to excellence have inspired me to embrace and clarify my own method and style. Every day that I walk into a classroom, I am grateful to be able to share my love of dance in the same spirit that my parents first shared dance with me: joyfully swinging together in rhythm. I hope this manual gives you many moments of swinging together with your students in a celebration of tap dance!

PART ONE: LEVELS

LEVEL I

AGES 6 & 7

STUDENT GOALS

Identify the two taps of the shoe and articulate the following single-sound movements: toe dig, heel drop, heel dig, toe drop, toe tip, brush, spank, heel stand, marching in place on the balls of the feet and stepping onto the ball of the foot with a relaxed, silent heel.

Be introduced to the Shuffle Series and Rudiment Series.

Identify the "1" and work exclusively in quarter-note time.

Perform a 64-bar (8-step) dance with minimal teacher direction.

Integrate the hands, head and voice into rhythm making.

Be introduced to technique that emphasizes the 3 R's:

Release: transfer weight fully so that there is always a foot in the ready position.

Relax: keep knees soft, ankles loose, weight over arch, skeleton stacked naturally.

Ready: hang one foot loosely from knee, which is lifted.

MUSICAL RHYTHMS

FOR GAMES, IMPROVISATION AND CHOREOGRAPHY

Goals

Identify the quarter note in ⁴/₄ and ³/₄ time and apply movements below in quarter-note time.

Hold or wait a quarter note; respect the "silent" note.

"Count" the notes of the movement.

Identify the "1."

"Play" the quarter notes through tapping, clapping and drumming. Encourage dancers to "show" the rhythm clearly through their hands, heads and voices. Post the rhythms on a wall or mirror. Have a dancer "play" the rhythm and other dancers guess the correct one. Notes in parentheses are silent.

1 2 3 4 (5 6 7 8)
1 2 3 (4) 5 6 7 (8)
1 (2) 3 (4) 5 (6) 7 (8)
(1) 2 (3) 4 (5) 6 (7) 8
(1) 2 3 (4 5) 6 7 8
1 2 (3) 4 (5) 6 (7) 8
1 2 (3) 4 5 (6) 7 8
1 2 (3) 4 (5) 6 7 (8)

CLASS OUTLINE - LEVEL I

The following class outline includes suggested tunes that will help teachers organize their weekly lessons. A brief description of what to do is provided. Particularly in Level I, it is important to establish a regular structure that enables students to progress systematically through the curriculum. Read through The Next Step, where more details about skill development are discussed. Refer to Part Two (The Series) for specific exercises for each skill. As the year progresses, modify the class outline and music to keep students challenged. See the lesson plan worksheet at the end of the manual.

Rudiments - center floor 👞See Rudiment Series (p. 87)
"Never Smile at a Crocodile" ("Tap x Three," Statler)
Dancers stand with R foot lifted and relaxed. In half-time, they press R toe dig down, then heel drop, then toe drop, then rock from heel to toe, then shift weight to change feet. Do 7 of each, then 3 of each, then 1.

Marching and Stepping - center floor
"Hey Look Me Over" ("Preschool Playtime Band," Kimbo)
"Consider Yourself" ("Preschool Aerobic Fun," Kimbo)
Dancers march on balls of feet for four marches and wait four counts with alternate leg lifting with a relaxed ankle. Use the terms *Ready* and *Release* to reinforce the full weight shift and the *Ready* foot. Repeat in combinations of two and wait two, one and wait one, then move to march three and wait one count. Week by week add ball taps, heel digs, toe tips and toe digs to marching

pattern. Move forward, back, side to side and in a square, emphasizing timing, staying on the balls while marching and resting the heel when standing and waiting. It will take time for young dancers to learn to rest their heel silently, but continue to emphasize "just the ball tap" when marching. With consistent practice and instruction, dancers will learn to relax their feet. Be careful that they are not locking their knees when standing on one foot. You can have dancers march their way to the barre for the next exercise. Be sure to have dancers march by themselves so they can learn to listen to their sounds. Are they using just their toe tap?

Shuffles - at the barre for brushing and spanking = shuffles ☛ See Shuffle Series (p. 121)
"Red Red Robin" ("Ready Set Dance," Statler) right side
"'A' You're Adorable" ("School House Tots," Statler) left side
Practice on one side at a time to develop muscle memory and strength. Holding the barre with one hand, use proper barre etiquette and placement, keeping weight over arches and hand forward to stack shoulder, hip, knee and ankle. Working leg should brush freely initially before finding the Ready position (knee lifted, with foot hanging in front with a relaxed ankle).

Combos, Across-the-Floor (ATF) patterns and Center-Floor Choreography
"Broadway Baby" ("Tap for Kids," Statler)
When practicing across-the-floor and center-floor choreography, be sure to incorporate upper body movement, including arms, hands, heads and voices, in learning the rhythms and applying new techniques. Refer to the Combos section that follows for specific combinations to build new skills and reinforce the techniques introduced in the warm-up.

Song and Dance for Level I
"Ya Know What" (artist unknown)
End class with a fun song-and-dance tune, incorporating new skills each week into the dance section.

More tunes for Level I tap fun!
"Polly Wolly Doodle" ("School House Tots," Statler)
"Satin Doll" ("Tap for Kids," Statler)
"Button Up Your Overcoat" ("Tap x Three," Statler)
"Bushel and a Peck" ("Ready Set Dance," Statler)
"Put on a Happy Face" ("Ready Set Dance," Statler)
"Side by Side" ("Tap x Three," Statler)
"Carolina" (Dean Martin)
"Don't Be a Do-Badder" (Bing Crosby)
"Take a Little One Step" ("Tap x Three," Statler)
"An Apple for the Teacher" ("School House Tots," Statler)
"McNamara's Band" ("Music for Tap Dancing," Kimbo)

THE NEXT STEP

The following skills, organized alphabetically, are introduced in Level I. Included are suggestions for when and how to teach these skills. Combinations for center-floor and across-the-floor work are included in the Combo section that follows. For specific weekly exercises based on rhythmic progressions, **see Part Two for the Shuffle Series and Rudiment Series** for Level I dancers.

Ball Taps - (tap) striking the toe tap to the floor with no weight while standing on one foot

This can be included in the marching part of the warm-up and is introduced in combination with steps. While keeping the knee and ankle soft and relaxed, and the toes flat in the shoe, dancers extend the working leg forward at a low angle. DO NOT encourage flexing and pointing, which lead to tense ankles. The whole leg lifts lightly with the toe tap landing slightly in front of the supporting leg. Make sure the supporting knee is not locked.

Brushes and Spanks - (br) (sp) brushing the toe tap on the floor

☛ **See Shuffle Series (p. 121)**
Brushes (forward) and spanks (backward) are introduced at the barre during the warm-up. When balance is not an issue, strength in both the working leg and the supporting leg improves through the weekly lessons.

Heel Digs - (hdig) hitting the back edge of the heel to the floor with no weight

Introduce the heel dig during the marching/stepping part of the warm-up. Make sure dancers are not locking their knees by encouraging them to place the heel dig slightly in front. Move slowly, ensuring that dancers lift the knee before and after the heel dig.

Heel Drops - (hdrp) isolating the flat heel sound

See Rudiment Series (p. 87)

Heel drops are incorporated into the opening Rudiment Series, which starts the warm-up. Emphasize soft knees and loose ankles. Be sure dancers are keeping their toes flat and grounded as they lift and lower just the heel. Heel drops begin to transfer weight as they are incorporated into across-the-floor movements when combined with steps and toe digs.

Heel Stands - (hstand) heel dig with weight

These can be taught center floor as part of choreography. Teach a heel stand once dancers have mastered the heel dig without a locked knee. The knee should remain soft when shifting weight fully to the heel dig. Some Level I dancers may not have the strength to stand on their heels yet, but this movement can be a nice "flashy" step and is very suited to waltz time. Practice center floor, standing on either one or two heel digs at a time.

Hops - (hop) from one foot to the same foot

Hops can be integrated into across-the-floor-patterns. At this level, dancers know how to hop from skipping in earlier years. The goal is to hop rhythmically on the ball of the foot and with volume and clarity. Challenge students to hop in quarter-note time. Have dancers listen carefully to hear the hopping sounds and play the correct rhythm.

Shuffles - (sh) brush + spank

See Shuffle Series (p. 121)

In Level I, shuffles are done as two separate movements. Perform in quarter-note time to assure technique and clarity. Suggest the image of painting a stripe on the floor and use hands and arms in big sweeping motions. As they master the ability to use just their toe tap and keep their heel off the floor, introduce the idea of keeping the action in front. The *Ready* Position (working leg lifted and slightly bent with relaxed foot and ankle hanging loosely from knee) will be used throughout their training, so continue to reinforce this concept regularly.

Steps - (st) transferring weight from foot to foot

Steps and marches are introduced during the second song of the warm-up. Both involve a complete transfer of weight. Emphasize stepping onto the ball of the foot, releasing the alternate foot, stepping/marching in time to the music with a designated number of repetitions. Combine steps with "waits" and single-sound movements like heel digs and toe tips. **The biggest challenge at this level is to help the dancer gain the strength to step onto the ball of the foot and silently lower the heel.** This may not happen until Level II, but continue to promote a quiet heel.

Toe Digs - (tdig) pressing/touching the flat toe tap to the floor with no weight

See Rudiment Series (p. 87)

This skill is introduced in the first Rudiment exercise and becomes strengthened weekly through practice. At this level, dancers do these next to and slightly in front of the standing foot. Emphasize the lift of the knee prior to the tap touching the floor and the energy going downward, not forward.

Toe Drops - (tdrp) dropping the flat toe tap to the floor with the heel in place

🔖 See Rudiment Series (p. 87)

These are introduced in the first Rudiment exercise and continue to be strengthened with weekly practice. Level I dancers can do these in parallel and turned out, in different rhythms, but generally do not fully shift weight.

Toe Tips - (tip) striking the tip of the toe tap to the floor with no weight

Toe tips are introduced center floor during the marching song, as they are done in combination with steps/marches. Make sure dancers are striking the floor with the absolute tip of the shoe and lifting it immediately. The toe tip is either placed straight back, crossed diagonally in back or crossed diagonally in front. Some teachers refer to a toe tip as a "knock."

COMBOS

The following combos can be used as drills, center-floor choreography, or across-the-floor patterns. They are samples of combinations that bring the Level I skills together. A common pattern of "three and a break" is frequently used. Add hand and head movements to reinforce the rhythms.

Ball Taps (tap)

+Steps:

```
1   2   3   4 5 6 7   8                1   2   3   4                1   2 3   4 5   6 7   8
tap tap tap .........(7x) st REVERSE   tap tap tap st REVERSE      tap st tap st tap st tap st
R   R   R             R                R   R   R   R                R   R L   L R   R L   L
```

Brushes and Spanks (br) (sp)

I do not use either the brush or the spank independently with other movements at this level. There is enough challenge in learning to combine these two movements into a clean shuffle, with the foot lifted and relaxed.

Heel Digs (hdig)

+Steps:

🎵 **Vocals:** "1... same foot, 2... same foot, 3...same foot, 4... change"

```
1 (2) 3 4     5 (6) 7 8     1 (2) 3 4     5 (6) 7 (8)
hdig  st st   hdig  st st   hdig  st st   hdig  st to change feet  REVERSE
R     R L     R     R L     R     R L     R     R RELEASE
```

+Hops:

🎵 **Vocals:** "Heel hop step step, heel hop step step, heel hop change, heel hop change"

```
1    2    3    4    5    6    7    8 1    2    3    (4) 5    6    7 (8)
hdig hop  st   st   hdig hop  st   st   hdig hop  st       hdig hop  st   REPEAT
R    L    R    L    R    L    R    L    R    L    R         L    R    L
```

+Toe tips: Place diagonally back behind the standing leg or cross in front

1	(2)	3 (4)	5	(6)	7	8			1	(2)	3 (4)	5	(6)	7	(8)
hdig		tip	hdig		st	st	(3x) and BREAK:		hdig		tip	hdig		st	RELEASE to REVERSE
R		R	R		R L				R		R	R		R	

Heel Drops (hdrp)

Begin with the exercises in the Traveling Rudiment Series Level I before teaching the following combos:

+Tdigs/Steps:

ATF: Step heel progressions with opposition arms and heads while traveling in circle/square/ around and across the room. Dancers at this level are not fully shifting weight on the toe dig. Encourage a complete shift with a release on the silent notes.

1	2	3	(4)	5	6	7	(8)	1	2	3	4	5	6	7	8	
tdig	hdrp	hdrp		tdig	hdrp	hdrp		tdig	hdrp	tdig	hdrp	march				RELEASE to REPEAT
R	R	R		L	L	L		R	R	L	L	R L R L				

+Toe Drops: In place and with small movement to side when ready.

Simple crawl:

1	2	3	4			1	2	3	(4)	
tdig	hdrp	tdrp	hdrp	REVERSE		tdig	hdrp	tdrp		REVERSE
R	R	R	R			R	R	R		

REPEAT both rhythms.

Heel Stands (hstand)

+Steps:

1		2	3 (4)	5		6	7(8)	1		2		3	4	5	(6)	7	(8)	
hstand		st	st	hstand		st	st	hstand		hstand		st	st	jump		jump		REPEAT or REVERSE
R		L	R	L		R L		R		L		R L		OUT		IN		

		1		2 3	4		5 6	1		2 3	4		5 6	
Waltz time (³/₄):		hstand	st st	hstand		st st		hstand	st st	hstand	st st			
		R		L R L			R L R			L R L			R L	

Hops

+Steps:

1	2	3	4	5	6	7	8
st	hop	st	st	st	hop	st	st
R	R	L	R	L	L	R	L

1	2	3	4	5	6	7	(8)	
st	hop	st	st	hop	st	st		RELEASE
R	R	L	R	R	L	R		

REVERSE ALL ABOVE

Shuffles (sh)

+Steps: REVERSE all combos - change direction

```
12 (3) (4)  56 (7) (8)  12 (3) (4)  5 6 7 (8)
sh wait wait  sh wait wait  sh wait wait  march  RELEASE to REVERSE
R            R            R            R L R
```

```
12 3 4      56 7 (8)
sh st st 3x  sh  st  RELEASE to REVERSE
R R L        R  R
```

```
1 2 34 5 6 78 1 2 34 5 6 7 (8)
st st sh st st sh st st sh st st st  RELEASE to REVERSE and change direction (side to side)
R L R R L R R L R R L R
```

Steps (st)

+Claps:

```
1 (2) 3 (4) 5 (6)7 (8)1 (2)3 (4) 5    (6 7 8)
st    clap st   clap st   clap clap  wait  REVERSE
R          L         R
```

```
1 (2) 3 (4) 5  6  7  (8)
st    st  st st st      3x  REVERSE  (Try traveling around the room or side to side.)
R     L   R  L  R
```
BREAK:
```
1  2    3 4   5 6   7  (8)
st clap  st clap  st clap clap
L        R        L
```

+Heel digs: Step on the ball and encourage dancers to rest the heel on count 4.

```
1  2  3  4  5    6  7   8
st st st st hdig st hdig st   (4x in a square)
R  L  R  L  R    R L     L
```

+Tips:

```
1 2 34 5 6 7 8 1 2 3 4 5 6 7 8
st st st tip st st st tip st tip st tip st tip st tip  (traveling side to side)
R L R L L R L R R L L R R L L R
```

Toe Digs (tdig)

+Steps: alternate the following two rhythms

```
1  2 3  45  6 7  8
tdig st tdig st tdig st tdig st
R  R L  L  L R R L  L
```

```
1   2 3  4
tdig st st st  REVERSE (traveling side to side)
R   R L R
```

Thelma's Notes

Include arm and head movements as well as the voice, so the rhythm becomes full-bodied.

+Heel drops: as the toe digs and heel drops travel, the toe dig eventually becomes a step. To help dancers remember to lift the knee, press downward, and articulate the full toe sound, use the words "*lift*" and "*press*."

♪ **ATF: Vocals:** "*lift press heel heel lift press heel heel lift press heel press heel   clap*"

(1)	2	3	4	(5)	6	7	8	(1)	2	3	4	5	(6)	7	(8)
	tdig	hdrp	hdrp		tdig	hdrp	hdrp		tdig	hdrp	tdig	hdrp			
	R	R	R		R	L	L		L	L	R	R		R	L	L

When the full alignment is:

```
    (1) 2    3    4   (5) 6    7    8   (1) 2    3    4   5  (6) 7  (8)
        tdig hdrp hdrp    tdig hdrp hdrp    tdig hdrp tdig hdrp
        R    R    R    R   L    L    L    L   R    R    R    L   L
```

When going across the floor, this is often referred to as "dig heel" or "step heel."

+Heel digs: Emphasize the weight shift on the last three heel drops.

```
1   (2) 3 (4) 5 (6) 7 (8) 1   (2) 3 (4) 5    6    7    (8)
hdig tdig hdig tdig    hdig tdig hdrp hdrp hdrp RELEASE to REVERSE
R    R    R    R       R    R    R    L    R
```

> Start on count 8: ★ **SIMPLE SHIM-SHAM RHYTHM:**
>
> ```
> 8 1   2 3   4 5   6    7
> (*) step (*) step (*) step step step REVERSE
> R R   L L   R R   L    R
> ```
> *insert toe dig, heel dig, toe tip or ball tap

Toe Drops (tdrp)

+Heel Digs: These can be done first in half-time to assure good technique (not locking knees).

Half-time: every 2 quarter notes
```
1   (2) 3   (4) 5   (6) 7 (8)
    hdig tdrp hdig tdrp
    R    R    L    L
```

```
      1    2    3    4    5    6    7    8
ATF: hdig tdrp hdig tdrp hdig tdrp hdig tdrp
      R    R    L    L    R    R    L    L
```

```
1    2    3 (4) 5    6    7 (8) 1         2 3 4 5    6 7 (8)
hdig tdrp st    hdig tdrp st    hstand st st st hstand st st    REVERSE
R    R    L     R    R    L      R      L R L R    L R
```

Toe Tips (tip)

+Steps: This combo can move in a square/circle.

```
1  2  3  4  5  6 7 8
st tip st tip st tip st tip REPEAT or continue with next phrase.
R  L  L  R  R  L  L R
```

```
1  2  3 4 5 6 7 8
st tip st st tip st st tip REVERSE (Add a head movement that follows the tip.)
R  L  L R L L R L
```

CHOREOGRAPHY IDEAS

VOCALIZE MOVEMENT AND "COUNTS"

Tap Routine - "My Dancing Doll" ("Oh, You Beautiful Doll," "Scotch Mist," Ray Sherman).

It's always fun to dance with a prop, especially when it's your favorite doll! This tune has no vocals so it's also a nice opportunity to supply their own voices to this standard song that's very appropriate for young tappers.

INTRO: Skip or chassé to places, holding doll with two hands at doll's waist, doll facing out to audience. Bounce with feet together.

Song and Movements:
"Oh, you beautiful doll, you great big beautiful doll"
Extend doll forward on lyrics: *oh, beau…, great, doll* (cts. 1, 5, 1, 5)

"Let me put my arms around you, I can never live without you"
Doll rocks right to left; to right on lyrics: *let, arms, I, live* (cts. 1, 5, 1, 5)

"Oh, you beautiful doll, you great big beautiful doll"
Extend doll forward on lyrics: *oh, beau…, great, doll* (cts. 1, 5, 1, 5)

"If you ever leave me how my heart will break"
Extend doll, step R to R on "*ever*" and bring doll back to chest, step L to R on "*heart*"

"I long to hold you but I fear you'll break"
Reverse above movement on "*long*" and "*fear*"

"Oh, oh, oh, oh, oh, you beautiful doll"
Extend doll up, to chest, to audience and then place on floor on each of the first four *ohs*, then march 4 and bounce in place.

STEP ONE: HEEL STEP, every other dancer moving back on marches to form 2 lines.
```
1    2 3 4    5 6 7    8
hdig st st hdig st  st  hdig  st    REVERSE and REPEAT 4x in all
R    R L R   R L R     R
```

STEP TWO: TIP, moving side to side with tip going to back.
```
1 2 3 4 5 6  7 8
st st st tip st tip st tip  REVERSE and REPEAT 4x in all
R L R L L  R R L
```

BREAK: This 16 ct. interlude is perfect for a change-line movement.
```
1 2 3 4 5 6 7 8                              12345678
st st st st st st st st  (march, changing lines; turn to face stage L and bounce 4x)
R L R L R L R L
```

STEP THREE: SHUFFLES, dancers facing stage L and then turning to stage R on cts. 5, 6, 7.

1 2 34 5 6 78 1 2 34 5 6 7 (8)

st st sh st st sh   st st sh   st st st RELEASE and REVERSE, facing stage R

R L R R L R   R L R R L R L

STEP FOUR: HEEL-TOE, dancers moving side to side.

1   2   3 4   5   6 7   8

hdig tdrp st hdig tdrp st hdig   tdrp   REVERSE and REPEAT 4x in all

R   R   L R   R   L R   R

BREAK (16 ct.): PRESS HEEL, dancers in row 2 moving forward to make one line.

1   2   3   4   5   6   7   8

tdig hdrp tdig hdrp tdig hdrp tidig hdrp

R   R   L   L   R   R   L   L

1 2 3 4 56   78

st st st st bend and pick up doll

R L R L

STEP FIVE: holding doll with two hands and extending doll to coincide with tapping foot.

1 2 3 4 5 6 7 8

tap tap tap tap tap tap tap st   REVERSE

R R R R R R R

1 2 3 4 5 6 7 8

tap tap tap st tap tap tap st

R R R R L L L L

1 2 3 4 5   (6)   7 (8)

tap st tap st extend doll up then hug to chest

R R L L

☻ SMILE!!!!!

IMPROVISATION ACTIVITIES

The goal at this level is for dancers to improvise for 1 bar (4 counts) of music, starting and ending on time. Playing "Call and Response" is very successful with young dancers, and using musical instruments to express a rhythm to copy is fun. Have dancers "play" a rhythm with their hands, a drum, lummi sticks, etc., and have partners copy the rhythm with their feet. Try having them use just their heels or just their toe taps.

LEVEL II

AGES 7 & 8

(Dancers who have completed Level I)

STUDENT GOALS

Learn the following tap movements: ball changes, slaps, double heel drops, press and regular cramp rolls, stamps, stomps and shuffles.

Continue to develop Shuffle and Rudiment Series and be introduced to the Double Heel Series and the Slap and Flap Series.

Dance in rhythms that include both straight and swinging eighth notes.

Perform a 64-bar dance with no teacher support.

Demonstrate good timing and integration of hands, heads and voices.

Learn simple Condos Rudiments.

Demonstrate increased understanding of the 3 R's: *Release, Relax, Ready*.

REVIEW

(INTRODUCED IN LEVEL I)

Reinforce single-sound movements; use in combinations and in duple time:

- ■ BRUSHES
- ■ HEEL DIGS
- ■ HEEL DROPS
- ■ HEEL STANDS
- ■ HOPS
- ■ SHUFFLES
- ■ SPANKS
- ■ STEPS
- ■ TIPS
- ■ TOE DIGS
- ■ TOE DROPS

MUSICAL RHYTHMS

FOR GAMES, IMPROVISATION AND CHOREOGRAPHY

Goals

Identify the quarter note and eighth note in $^4/_4$ and $^3/_4$ time and apply movements to the rhythms below.
Hold or wait a quarter note, respecting the "silent" note.
"Count" the notes of the movement.
Identify the "1."
"Play" the following rhythms, which incorporate quarter notes, eighth notes and eighth-note triplets, through tapping, clapping and drumming.

STRAIGHT RHYTHMS
1&2&3&4 5 6 7 8
1 2 3 4 5&6&7&8&
1&2 3&4 5&6 7&8
1 2 3&4 5 6 7&8
1&2 3 4&5 6 7&8

SWINGING RHYTHMS
1a2a3a4 5 6 7 8
1 2 3 4 5a6a7a8
1a2 3a4 5a6 7a8
1 2 3a4 5 6 7a8
1a2 3 4a5 6 7a8

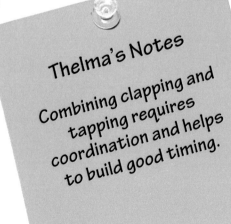

Thelma's Notes

Combining clapping and tapping requires coordination and helps to build good timing.

24

CLASS OUTLINE - LEVEL II

The following class outline includes suggested tunes that will help teachers organize their weekly lessons. A brief description of what to do is provided. As in Level I, it is important to establish a regular structure that enables students to progress systematically through the curriculum. Read through The Next Step, where more details about skill development are discussed. Refer to Part Two (The Series) for specific exercises for each skill. See the lesson plan worksheet at the end of the manual.

Rudiments - center floor ➤See The Rudiment Series (p. 87)
"I've Got the Sun in the Morning" ("Tap for Kids," Statler)
Stagger your dancers in one or two lines across the floor, with R leg lifted in the Ready position. Start with 7 toe digs, then heel drops, then toe drops, then rock from heel to toe. Change feet. Start at half time to ensure good technique, then move to quarter-note time. By the end of the year, dancers should be able to do 8, 4 and 1 of each with clean transitions.

Rudiments/Cramp Rolls/Press Cramp Rolls - center floor
➤See Double Heel Series (p. 105)
"Oobabaloo" (Fred Penner)
This tune has a very straight feel and is perfect for teaching step and heel drop combos, including Condos Rudiments that move from side to side, cramp rolls and press cramp rolls. Say *"press"* to aid dancers in shifting weight and Releasing other foot as the heel drops. Work in half time to promote good technique. Ensure dancers are playing accurate quarter notes and are moving side to side and forward and back with clean, distinct toe-dig and heel-drop combinations. As dancers master toe dig/step heel rudiments, move to simple cramp roll exercises during this tune. Eventually, once ball changes are mastered, the cramp roll rhythm moves from straight quarter notes [1 2 3 4] to swinging eighth notes [a1 (&) a2].

Ball Changes (BC) - at the barre
"Strike Up the Band" ("Preschool Band," Kimbo) BC exercises on the right
"Consider Yourself" ("Oliver," Broadway original cast) BC exercises on the left
Always review proper barre placement. Dancers face the barre for ball changes. Begin with march, march, wait, ball change [1 2 (3) a4], saying *"slow slow wait go quick"* or *"right left... right left."* This is a fun opportunity for the dancers to vocalize phrases like: *"I like...to TAP!"* Be sure dancers are pushing off from the left foot. As dancers master the technique, shift to doing just ball changes with a wait [a1(2 3 4)] then [a1(2) a3 (4)] and then 2 ball changes with a wait [a1 a2 (3 4)] and 3 BC [a1a2a3 (4)] with a wait. As dancers progress during the year, add single sounds like heel digs, toe tips and toe digs to ball change exercises at the barre.

Shuffles - at the barre ➤See Shuffle Series (p. 121)
"Orange Colored Sky" ("Tap for Kids," Statler) Right side
"I've Got No Strings" (Barbra Streisand) Left side
Review barre etiquette as dancers shift to face the side, reminding them to use only one hand on the barre. Begin with brushes and spanks in quarter-note time, reviewing Ready position and assuring that ankles and knees are Relaxed and not locked. Begin with a brush, wait, spank, wait [1 (2) 3 (4)] then proceed to a quarter-note shuffle [1 2 (3 4)]. Ensure that swing is relaxed and that only the toe tap brushes the floor and begins and ends in the Ready position. Follow the progressive exercises in the Shuffle Series to build strength and control, eventually doing two swinging shuffles [a1 a2 (3 4)].

Slaps - center floor ☛See Slap and Flap Series (p. 135)
"Satin Doll" (Beegie Adair)
Do not rush into this until the previous warm-up patterns are in place and students have completed a review of all Level I skills and are progressing with ball changes and swinging shuffles. Have dancers stand in Ready position, brush out and tap down [1 (2) 3 (4)] and then [1 2(34)], always returning quietly (do not scrape toe tap) to Ready position. Be sure dancers are firmly placing toe tap on the floor and that knee is not locked, although it is reaching forward or to side as dancers progress. Use action words like "*con-nect*" and "*go down*" to reinforce the rhythm and power of a slap.

Combos, Across-the-Floor (ATF) patterns and Center-Floor choreography
"Getting to Know You" ("Ready Set Dance," Statler)
Refer to the Level II Combos for specific combinations to build new skills and reinforce the techniques introduced in the warm-up.

More tunes for Level II tap fun!
"Doodlin" (Germaine Salsberg)
"Button Up Your Overcoat" ("Tap X Three," Statler)
"Syncopated Clock" (Leroy Anderson)
"I Love My Piano" ("Music For Tap Dancing," Kimbo)
"Sunny Side of the Street" (Erroll Garner)
"Surrey With the Fringe on Top" ("Music For Tap Dancing," Kimbo)
"Rhythm in My Nursery Rhymes" ("School House Tots," Statler)
"An Apple for the Teacher" ("School House Tots," Statler)
"The Bare Necessities" (Tony Bennett)
"High Hopes" (Frank Sinatra)
"Ain't She Sweet" ("Tap Those Feet," Statler)
"Ballin' the Jack" ("Tap x Three," Statler) - a nice song-and-dance tune for Level II.

THE NEXT STEP

The following skills, organized alphabetically, are introduced in Level II. The Class Outline indicates when to teach them. Combinations for center-floor and across-the-floor work are included in the Combo section that follows. For specific weekly exercises based on rhythmic progressions, **see Part Two for the Shuffle Series, Slap and Flap Series, Double Heel Series and Rudiment Series for Level II dancers**.

Ball Changes - (BC) step + step

I like to introduce ball changes at the barre, following the Rudiment Series and before the shuffles. It's a natural progression from the marching that followed the Rudiments in Level I. It is important that dancers understand the difference between a ball change (using the balls of the feet) and a stamp stamp (flat foot). With two hands on the barre, dancers stay on the balls of the feet, head up, always returning to Ready position (foot relaxed and hanging in front). Practice the sequence of rhythms below. ALWAYS REVERSE! Watch for dancers who are weak on one side; help them to "push off" so the first step of the ball change becomes almost a "leap." Take your time in teaching this concept and ensure that dancers are picking up their feet and lifting knees high! Make it fun!

Teaching Ball Changes:
When teaching **ball changes**, it is important to discuss the idea of quietly lowering the "silent" heel to the floor for balance and stability. While emphasizing the ball sounds of the ball change, reinforce the relaxation of the foot so that when the ball change is completed and the dancer must stand on one foot to complete a shuffle or a slap, for instance, she/he has stability in the supporting leg. I refer to the lowering of the heel as the "silent" heel and associate it with the silent "e" at the end of a word; both are necessary but cannot be heard. With practice, the dancers will find that neutral stand over the arch that will result in clarity and strength in their ball-change patterns.

AT THE BARRE:
```
1       2       a3      (4 = back to Ready Position)
march march BC
```

Rhythm progressions:
```
1 2 a3 a4 .......
a1 (2) a3 (4)......
a1 a2 (3  4)
a1 a2 a3 (4)
```

Begin with ball changes in place, then in back, then to side.

Cramp Rolls - (CRRL) step step hdrp hdrp (4 sounds)

➤ See Double Heel Series (p. 105)

Cramp rolls can be taught as an extension of the step, heel-drop exercises in the Level II Rudiment Series. The Level II cramp-roll rhythms to teach are: [1 2 3 4], [1&2&], [a1 (2) a3], [a1 a2]. Specific teaching tips are discussed in the Double Heel Series. Focus on separating sounds and articulating each one fully. ALWAYS REVERSE.

Line Step: This is a great skill to drill individually down the line, with each dancer doing:
```
1234    5&6&    7&8&    1234    5&6&    7   (8)
CRRL    CRRL    CRRL    CRRL    CRRL    st
RLRL    RLRL    RLRL    RLRL    RLRL    R       REVERSE
```

Press Cramp Rolls - tdig hdrp hdrp (3 sounds)

See Double Heel Series for detailed exercises (p. 105)
These can be taught at the same time as regular cramp rolls. Dancers begin with toe dig in place, then drop heel, then shift to drop other heel. Work in quarter-note time with emphasis on shifting weight from one heel to the other and releasing/lifting the heel, saying *"press, lift, lift, release"* for repetitions on the same foot, building strength in the supporting leg as they build coordination and facility in the working leg. As dancers practice working in place, they can extend the toe dig to the side. As they master the technique of shifting weight and *Releasing* the *Ready* foot, they can begin to work at faster tempos, eventually working in duple and swing time.

Shuffles - (sh) brush + spank, develop two swinging shuffles

See Shuffle Series for specific progressions and teaching tips (p. 121)
As indicated in the Class Outline, shuffles can follow the ball change exercises in the warm-up. Review barre etiquette: one hand on the barre and joints stacked properly with a soft knee in the supporting leg. Begin and end in *Ready* position with ankle relaxed, knee lifted with foot hanging loosely. Always start with clear, articulate quarter-note brushes and spanks, keeping the movement in front of the dancer. As dancers progress through levels, it will be very important that they don't automatically spank every time they brush out! Teach your dancers to send the foot out and leave it there to build strength and isolate the single sound before combining it with a spank for shuffles.

To increase tempo and strength, begin with:
"slow, slow, wait, quick, quick" [1 2 (3) a4]
"slow, slow, slow, quick" [1 2 3& (4)]

Slaps - (sl) brush + tap (no weight)

See Slap and Flap Series (p. 135)
Slaps can be taught following the shuffle series. With one hand on the barre, begin in *Ready* position, brush out and tap down; begin in quarter-note time and, when sounds are clear, double up, progressing from [1 2 (3 4)] to [a1 (2) a3 (4)]. Dancers perform to front and open to side, returning foot silently to *Ready* position on "2" and "4." Use a word like *"con-nect!"* to emphasize the two sounds.

Flaps (which transfer weight) are not recommended for young Level II dancers. Focus on the strong "connection" with the floor and the swinging rhythm of slaps.

Stamps - (STA) full foot, single sound with transfer of weight, sometimes accented

I often introduce stamps during the rudiment warm-up as another "single" sound we can make with our taps. Be careful to have dancers lower the whole foot flat to the floor with a weight shift. It will take time and practice to avoid rolling the foot or stamping too loudly. Stamps are a great way to teach accented sounds.

Stomps - (STO) full foot, single sound with no transfer of weight

A stomp is a flat, full-footed placement on the floor without a weight shift. These can be taught during warm-up as another single sound dancers can make with their taps. As with stamps, the teacher must be careful that dancers are lowering the full foot to the floor and not separating their toe and heel sounds. Look in the Combo section for choreography ideas that combine stomps with toe drops.

COMBOS

The following combos can be used as drills, center-floor choreography or across-the-floor patterns. They are samples of combinations that bring the Level I and II skills together. When combining different movements, be sure that dancers are *Ready* to execute the desired movement. Note that many of the following combos have a wait on count 8, so that dancers can transition and be *Ready* for what's next. In all combos, add arms and head movements so that dancers are moving with style and bringing the rhythm into their full body.

Ball Changes (BC)

In combination with most single sounds learned in Level I:

+Steps: (*Release* the foot to *Ready* position on the clap) - the steps and the ball changes in this combo can be in place, behind or open to second, or can be alternately "out" or "in," or can travel.

```
1 2    a3  4 5    a6  a7  8
st st  BC  st st  BC  BC  clap  3x in all
R L    RL  R L    RL  RL  RELEASE
```

BREAK:
```
a1  2    a3  4    a5  6   7     (8)
BC  clap BC  clap BC  st  tdig  RELEASE
RL       RL       RL  R   L     L
```

REVERSE ALL ABOVE

+Heel digs:
```
1     a2  3    a4  5    a6  7    8
hdig  BC  hdig BC  hdig BC  hdig st   REVERSE
R     RL  R    RL  R    RL  R    R
```

+Toe Tips:
```
1   2   a3  4   5 6   a7  8   1   2   a3  4   a5  6   a7  8
st  tip BC  tip st tip BC tip st  tip BC  tip BC  tip BC  tip  REVERSE
R   L   LR  L   L  R   RL R   R   L   LR  L   LR  L   LR  L
```

+Shuffles:
```
a1(2) a3 (4) a5 (6) a7 (8) a1  a2 (3) a4 a5  a6   7  (8)
sh    BC    sh    BC     sh  BC     sh  BC  BC  st  RELEASE to REVERSE
R     RL    R     RL     R   RL     R   RL  RL  R
```

Cramp Rolls (CRRL)

Level II rhythms and words/phrases to help build clarity:
[1 2 3 4] *"I like to dance"*
[1&2&] *"Watermelon"*
[a1 a2] *"Vanilla cream"*

Thelma's Notes

Include one-at-a-time and down-the-line activities, so dancers have an opportunity to listen to themselves.

Combine with:

+Steps: this combo can travel by stepping to the right and then staying in place for the cramp roll. Vocalize the rhythm by saying:

"One scoop vanilla cream, two scoops vanilla cream, three scoops vanilla cream…"

1	2	a3a4		5	6	a7a8		1	2	a3a4
st	st	CRRL		st	st	CRRL		st	st	CRRL
R	L	RLRL		R	L	RLRL		R	L	RLRL

…I want sprinkles"

```
          5   6   7   8
BREAK: hit hit  clap snap  REVERSE
```
(hit knees with both hands, clap and then snap)

+Heel Digs: be clear as to whether you want to swing or be straight!

```
1    2&3&  4   5&6&  7    8  - straight
1    a2a3  4   a5a6  7    8  - swing
hdig CRRL hdig CRRL hdig st    REVERSE
R    RLRL  R   RLRL R    R
```

Press Cramp Rolls

In teaching these phrases, use the word "*press*" to reinforce the toe-dig sound.
Level II rhythms and words/phrases to help build clarity:

[1 2 3 (4)] "*Ice cream cone*"
[1 & 2] "*Cantaloupe*"
[1 a2] "*Popsicle*"

```
1    &    2    3    &    4    5    &    6    7    8  - straight
1    a    2    3    a    4    5    a    6    7    8  - swing
tdig hdrp hdrp tdig hdrp hdrp tdig hdrp hdrp tdig hdrp  RELEASE to REVERSE
R    R    L    R    R    L    R    R    L    R    R
Out            In             Out            In
```

Shuffles (sh)

Shuffles continue to be a primary movement idea and are an important part of Level II development. Use them in combinations with steps, toe digs and ball changes. Always emphasize the completion of the shuffle by using phrases like "*finish*" [1&] and "*attack*" [a1]. **Just as important**: make sure the shuffle is beginning from a *Relaxed, Ready* position. Remind dancers to *Release* to *Ready* when they step before a shuffle.

+Steps: This combo can turn side to side or back to front on steps.

```
a1 (2) a3 (4) a5  6  7  8
sh    sh     sh st st st  RELEASE to REVERSE
R     R      R  R  L  R
```

+Press Cramp Roll: Be sure to emphasize the *Release* on the last heel drop.

```
a1 2  a   3    a4 5   a   6   7    8
sh tdig hdrp hdrp sh tdig hdrp hdrp tdig hdrp  RELEASE to REVERSE
R  R   R    L    R  R   R    L    R    R
```

+Toe Dig: This is a variation of one of the Condos Rudiments that will be developed in Level III.

```
1& 2   &   3  4   5   &   6   &  7   8
sh tdig hdrp tdig hdrp tdig hdrp tdig hdrp tdig hdrp  RELEASE to REVERSE
R  R   R    L   L   R   R    L   L   R    R
```

+Ball Change:

```
a1 a2 a3 (4) a5 a6  a7 (8) a1 a2 a3  4  5   (6 ) a7 (8)
sh sh BC     sh sh BC      sh sh BC st clap      BC   RELEASE to REVERSE
R  R  RL     R  R  RL      R  R  RL R            LR
```

```
12 a3  4  56 a7  8 12 a3  a4  5 (6) a7 a8
sh BC st sh BC st sh sh BC st    sh BC  RELEASE to REVERSE
R  RL R  L  LR L  R  R  RL R     L  LR
```

Slaps (sl)

+Step: In the combo below, the steps can move back, side, close together or half-turn to the back. Add diagonal arms that stop precisely on the "1," "3" and "5" for increased rhythmic expression.

```
a1 (2) a3 (4)a5 (6) 7  8  a1(2) a3 (4)  5  6  7 (8)
sl    sl     sl     st st sl    sl       st st st  RELEASE to REVERSE
R     R      R      R  L  R     R        R  L  R
```

Flaps (which transfer weight) are not recommended for young Level II dancers. Focus on the strong "connection" with the floor and the swinging rhythm of slaps. When that is mastered in Level II, dancers will transition smoothly to flaps in Level III. **There is no need to rush.**

Stamps (STA)

```
1 (2) 3 4                     5   6    7    (8)
STA tip st  3x  then BREAK: STA clap clap   RELEASE to REVERSE
R    L L                     R
```

```
1    2 3 4  5   6 7 8  1    2  a3  4 (5) a6 7    (8)
STA tip st tdig STA tip st tdig STA tip BC  tdig  BC tdig   RELEASE to REVERSE
R    L L R  R   L L R  R   L  LR L      LR L
```

Stomps (STO)

```
1 (2) 3  4  5 (6) a7 a8  1  (2)  3 4  5   (6) a7 8
STO st st STO  BC BC STO  st st STO   BC st REVERSE
R   RL R  R      RL RL R      R  L R      RL R
```

31

CHOREOGRAPHY IDEAS

A Level II tap dance should include a variety of simple rhythms and patterns that can be executed with clarity and confidence. Music choices should have a clear quarter note with simple or no lyrics. Encourage students to:

Vocalize steps and be able to sing and count rhythms.

Memorize a two-chorus dance that integrates movement in space (changing lines and formations) and listening to other dancers through "Call and Response."

Perform with style, confidence, clarity and good timing with minimal teacher direction.

Tap Routine - *"Doop Doo De Doop"* (Blossom Dearie)

INTRO: 16 cts. Start on stage or walk to one line upstage and bounce in place.

STEP ONE: Move forward together, in one line with arms at low diagonal.
```
1    2     3    4     5    6     7    a8
st   tdig  st   tdig  st   tdig  st   BC   3x, ending downstage
R    L     L    R     R    L     L    RL
```

BREAK:
```
1   (2) 3        4     (5) 6        7      (8)
STO     tdrp out tdrp in   tdrp out tdrp in   Move head with foot.
R       R        R         R        R
```

STEP TWO:
```
1 2   3 4    5 6    a7 a8
st hdrp st hdrp st hdrp BC BC   Travel R, then REVERSE to L.
R R   L L    R R    LR LR
```

BREAK:
```
1 2    a3 4   5 6 a7 8
st hdrp BC st   REPEAT
R R    LR L
```

```
1              2 3 4                        5 (6 )      7 (8)
```
close R to L and point R finger 3x across audience, open arms,   place hands on hips
AST: say   "2 3   4,   *like it so much, we'll show you some more!"*

STEP THREE: Every other dancer moves back or stays in place, hands on hips:
```
1    2 3   4 5   a6 7   a8
hdig st hdig st hdig BC hdig BC   3x
R    R L   L R   RL R   RL
```

32

BREAK:
```
1    2   a3  4  (5)  a6  7   8
hdig st  BC  st.... BC  st  st  Open BC to second position both times, then step together.
R    R   LR  L       RL  R   L
```

STEP FOUR: Stay in place (step can be changed to one shuffle with a pause before the BC).
```
a1   a2  a3  (4)   a5  a6  a7  (8)
sh   sh  BC...     sh  sh  BC
R    R   RL        R   R   RL
```

```
a1   a2  a3  a4  a5  a6  7   (8)
sh   sh  BC  sh  sh  BC  st   RELEASE to REVERSE all 16 cts.
R    R   RL  R   R   RL  R
```

STEP FIVE: Arms push out in opposition/diagonal with slap and open for shuffle.
```
a1 (2) a3 (4) a5  6   7   8                                a1(2)a3(4)a5678
sl     sl     sh  st  st  st (st st st travels back, side, close)   REVERSE
R      R      R   R   L   R
```

```
a1   2   3   4                                a5 6 7 8
sh   st  st  st   (travels back side close)   REVERSE
R    R   L   R                                L  L R L
```

BREAK:
```
1       2 3 4 5 6                    7     8
clap -  st st st st st together, jump out - in (change lines on steps)
        R L R L R
```

STEP SIX: Arms open for tip BC and drop to low diagonal for "*ooo-aah.*"
```
1  2  a3 4  5  6  a7 8  1  2  a3 4  5  6      7     8
st tip BC tip st tip BC tip st tip BC tip st  st (tog) tdrp  tdrp (say "ooo-aah" as both toes turn R to L)
R  L  LR L  L  LR RL R  R  L  LR L  L  R        both  both
```

REPEAT ALL ABOVE

STEP SEVEN: Arms work in opposition when hitting edge of opposite foot in front.
```
1    2       3   4       5  6   7    8
st   tip (back) st   hit (front) st  hdig st    st  REVERSE
R    L       L   R       R  L    L    R
```
4x in all. (Or do 3x and REPEAT vocal "*2 3 4, like it so much, we'll show you some more!*")

STEP EIGHT: Repeat Step One, back line moves forward to join front line.
```
1    2   3  4  5 6   7  a8
st   tdig st tdig st tdig st BC  3x
R    L   LR RL L  RL
```

```
1                    2   3       4  5                        6    7   (8)
Step R next to L.
AST:         say "All Through!"  clap clap  arms lift to high "V" while saying "Thank You!"
```

33

IMPROVISATION ACTIVITIES

The goal in Level II is for dancers to be able to improvise for two bars of music, to start on "1" and end on "8" and to follow simple directions regarding using just-toe or just-heel sounds. As in Level I, "Call and Response" is a great way for dancers to experiment with different ways to make rhythms. Nursery rhymes are an excellent motivator for improvising at this age; dancers can tap out the simple phrases of the rhymes. Good ones to use are:

"Three blind mice, three blind mice. See how they run, see how they run."
"The farmer in the dell, the farmer in the dell, heigh-ho the merry-o, the farmer in the dell."
"Old McDonald had a farm, e-i-e-i-o...."
"B-i-n-g-o, B-i-n-g-o, B-i-n-g-o and Bingo was his name-o!"

Have one dancer tap out a rhyme and have other dancers try to name it.

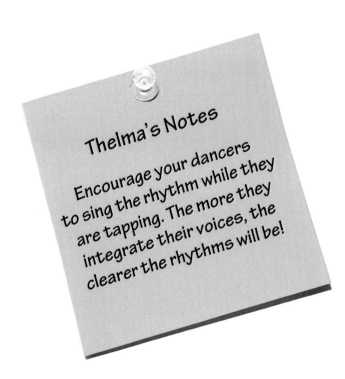

Thelma's Notes

Encourage your dancers to sing the rhythm while they are tapping. The more they integrate their voices, the clearer the rhythms will be!

LEVEL III

AGES 8 & 9

(Dancers who have completed Levels I & II)

STUDENT GOALS

Learn to shuffle in all directions: parallel, crossed, side and back. Be able to do three swinging shuffles followed by hops, ball changes and steps.

Continue to practice exercises described in the Rudiment Series, Shuffle Series, Slap and Flap Series and Double Heel Series.

Learn classic tap steps: Varsity Drag, Irish, Maxie Ford, Waltz Clog.

Learn to flap, leap, scuff and accent certain sounds.

Listen to own sounds and be able to self-correct.

Fully shift weight on rudiments; demonstrate increased understanding of the 3 R's: *Release, Relax* and *Ready*.

Perform a 64-bar dance with no teacher assistance and complex staging patterns, including canons, "Call and Response" and partner work.

.

REVIEW

MUSICAL RHYTHMS

FOR GAMES, IMPROVISATION AND CHOREOGRAPHY

Goals

Understand "swing" rhythm (triplets = 1&a2&a3...)
Create rhythms with syncopated sounds (accenting the "&" or "a" counts)
Find the "1" in standard swing, straight and waltz tunes
"Sing" the rhythm and participate in "Call and Response" activities

By clapping, drumming, tapping or other body percussion, the teacher plays the following rhythms and posts them on the wall or mirror. The teacher then repeats each rhythm, and the dancers identify the correct phrase. Once the dancers understand the challenge, they lead the game. The rhythmic challenge can be increased as the year progresses.

QUARTER NOTES
1 2 3 (4 5) 6 (7 8)
(1 2 3) 4 5 (6) 7 8

EIGHTH NOTES
1 2&3 4 5 6&7 8
1 2 3&4 5 6 7&8

EIGHTH-NOTE TRIPLETS
1(&)a2(&)a3(&)a4 5 6 7(&)a8
I&a2&a3(&)a4 - *"Lions and tigers and bears, oh my!"*

Thelma's Notes

Say the notes aloud to reinforce clarity and understanding of straight and swing rhythms.

CLASS OUTLINE - LEVEL III

The following class outline includes suggested tunes that will help teachers to organize their weekly lessons. A brief description of what to do is provided. By now, dancers are accustomed to the order of the class, and they appreciate the weekly attention to new skills. This regular structure enables students to progress systematically through the curriculum. Read through The Next Step, where more details about skill development are discussed. Refer to Part Two (The Series) for specific exercises. See the lesson plan worksheet at the end of the manual.

Rudiments - center floor ☛See Rudiment Series (p. 87)
"Peanut" (Maria Muldaur)
With R foot in Ready position, dancers follow the toe dig, heel drop, toe drop exercises outlined in the Rudiment Series. Continue with step-heel exercises that shift weight.

Cramp Rolls and more - center floor ☛See Double Heel Series (p. 105)
"Hugga-Hugga" (Gary Rosen)
"11 Long Years" (Us 3) Additional tune for duple step-heel work.
More rudiments; move from quarter to eighth notes, traveling side to side and forward and back. This is a great opportunity for a "down the line" exercise where each dancer does the exercise alone and the next dancer has to come in on the right note. Always shift and start on the left as often as the right.

Shuffles - at the barre ☛See Shuffle Series (p. 121)
"'A,' You're Adorable" (John Lithgow) Brushes, spanks and shuffles, right side
"A Bushel and a Peck" (Maria Muldaur) Left side
As in Levels I and II, progress slowly, treating brushes and spanks as individual skills as well as combining them for shuffles. This level is where to introduce "crossing" the shuffle: to the Level II series add a cross in front. Always introduce a movement in quarter-note time and progress only when dancers are displaying good technique and placement, ultimately increasing tempo to swinging shuffles. Dancers should progress to 3 swinging shuffles and should add ball changes, as in: [sh sh sh BC] and [sh sh BC BC], as described in the Shuffle Series.

Slaps and Flaps - at the barre ☛See Slap and Flap Series (p. 135)
"Jeepers Creepers" (Maria Muldaur)
Beginning with R foot in Ready position, review slaps to front and to side. Once slap is swinging and stopping rhythmically, first slowly in quarter-note time and then swinging the eighth notes, add heel drops, as discussed in the Double Heel Series. Begin teaching flaps as an extension of the slap. With dancers in Ready position, slap and move body forward to the ball of the foot, then step back to the ball of the other foot. Say, *"Go there and back,"* working in half time before progressing in tempo, eventually swinging the flaps forward with an alternate step, as in [a1 2 a3 4 a5 6 a7 8]. As dancers are able to work at the barre rhythmically, move them away and then return to the barre and reverse. End with flaps around the room in random patterns.

1 a2 a3

Ball Changes - center floor
"MacNamara's Band" (*"Preschool Playtime Band,"* Kimbo)
Ball changes continue to be drilled and combined with tips, heel digs, toe digs and shuffles. The following pattern can help to build strength and coordination. As dancers master the articulations and are staying on the balls of their feet, change the tune to increase tempo. Ball changes in Level III move to the front and the side as well as the back.

a. 1 2 a3 (4)   5 6 a7 8
    st st BC   3x   st st BC st   REVERSE
    R L RL   R L RL R

b. 1   a2 3   a4 5   a6 7   8
    hdig BC hdig BC hdig BC hdig st REVERSE
    R   RL R   RL R   RL R   R
    REPEAT above phrase substituting tip, toe dig and shuffle in place of the heel dig.

c. REPEAT "**b.**" with only one of each and then change feet.

d. REPEAT the following pattern with the ball change being placed back, then to the side, then to the front.
    1 2 a3 4 5 6 a7 8
    st st BC st st st BC st   REPEAT
    R L RL R L R LR L

Once mastered, increase the challenge with the following pattern. Alternate the placement of each ball change within the 8 counts (back, side, front) for an added challenge.
1 2 a3 4 a5 6 a7 8
st st BC st BC st BC st   REVERSE
R L RL R LR L RL R

Combos, Across-the-Floor (ATF) patterns and Center-Floor choreography
"Mairzy Doats" (Maria Muldaur)
Refer to the Combos section that follows for specific combinations to build new skills and reinforce the techniques introduced in the warm-up.

More tunes for Level III tap fun!
"Jada" (*"Music for Tap Dancing,"* Kimbo)
"Steppin' Out" (Fred Astaire)
"Chattanooga Choo Choo" (*"Dana's Best Sing & Swing-A-Long Tunes!"*)
"Smile" (*"Dana's Best Sing & Swing-A-Long Tunes!"*)
"Tea for Two" (Bobby Morganstein Productions)
"Side by Side" (Kay Starr)
"Zip-a-Dee-Doo-Dah" (Little Richard)
"Aren't You Glad You're You?" (Ella Fitzgerald)
"Play a Simple Melody" (*"Music for Tap Dancing,"* Kimbo)
"Dance if It Makes You Happy" (*"The Tap Dance Kid,"* Broadway original cast)
"Tap Tap" (*"The Tap Dance Kid,"* Broadway original cast)

THE NEXT STEP

The following skills, organized alphabetically, are introduced in Level III. The Class Outline indicates when to teach them. Combinations for center-floor and across-the-floor work are included in the Combo section that follows. For specific weekly exercises based on rhythmic progressions, **see Part Two for the Shuffle Series, Slap and Flap Series, Double Heel Series and Rudiment Series for Level III dancers**.

Ball Changes - (BC)

Take these to center floor after the Slap and Flap Series. Continue to emphasize the "ball" sound and combine with steps, heel digs, toe tips, toe digs and shuffles. Move the ball changes to the front as well as back, side and in, as detailed in the class outline.

Brushes and Spanks - (br) (sp)

Continue to develop brushes and spanks as individual motions during the Shuffle Series. In Level III, each of these movements is done diagonally, as well as open to the side. The following rhythm phrases can be added to the progressive exercises in the Level III Shuffle Series.
➜See Shuffle Series for further explanation and examples (p. 121)

1   (2)   3   (4)   5   (6)   7   (8)
br   wait   sp [crossed] wait   br forward wait   sp to *Ready* position
Practice the same sequence of movements with the following rhythms.
1 (2) 3 (4 5) 6 7 (8)
1   2 (3)a4 5   6   (7) a8
a1 a2 (3) a4 a5 (6) a7 a8

Cramp Rolls - (CRRL)

Teach these following the initial Rudiment Series warm-up. New rhythms include [1&a2] and [12a3].
➜See Double Heel Series (p. 105)   Continue to develop press cramp rolls.

Flaps - (fl) brush + step with weight change

➜See Slap and Flap Series (p. 135)
Teach these at the barre to assure good technique. The goal at this level is to develop clarity to master three consecutive flaps [a1 a2 a3 (4)] and flap ball change patterns, as in:

★**VARSITY DRAG:** flap step, flap step, flap step, flap BC [a1 2 a3 4 a5 6 a7 a8]

Leaps - transfer weight by pushing off from one foot to the other foot

Scuffs - (sc) strike the heel while swinging it forward

Introduce at the barre to assure good technique. Start in Ready position and swing the foot forward, striking only the heel. These can be taught following the shuffle drills.

Shuffles - (sh)

See Shuffle Series (p. 121)

Continue to develop good technique by working at the barre to build stamina and muscle memory. Always start with quarter-note phrasing to develop control and clarity, and always reinforce a Relaxed ankle, leg and hip. New shuffle skills at this level include increasing tempo, three consecutive shuffles, crossing the shuffle, adding a hop and adding a leap. Continue to emphasize lifting the knee and starting from a Ready position.

★ **MAXIE FORD:** step shuffle leap tip [1 a2 a3 (4)] (The Maxie Ford may also begin with a leap.)

★ **IRISH:** shuffle hop step [a1 a2]

★ **WALTZ CLOG:** step shuffle BC [1 a2 a3]

TEACHING WALTZ CLOG

First practice in ⁴/₄: 1   a2   a3   (4)
                        st   sh   BC   wait

³/₄ Time: 1   a2   a3   4   a5   a6
           st   sh   BC st   sh   BC

Other waltz steps for beginners in ¾ time: all [1 2 3]

step brush hop
step tap tap, or step dig dig, or step tip tip
step spank tip
step tip hop
step heel stand step

1 a2 a3 4

Slaps - (sl)

◄─ See Slap and Flap Series (p. 135)

In Level III, slaps progress to include an underneath heel drop and a double heel drop; they become flaps when weight is added.

Stomps - (STO)

Emphasize the single flat sound and the "no-weight" in preparation for time steps in Level IV. Practice in combination with ball changes and hops.

Stamps - (STA)

Emphasize the single flat sound and the shift in weight. Use alternately with steps to introduce the concept of accents.

Steps - (st)

◄─ See Rudiment Series (p. 87)

Emphasize the weight shift to the ball of the foot and the *Release* of the alternate foot. Dancers work in quarter-note, then eighth-note time and add heel drops, shuffles, flaps and more.

COMBOS

The following combos combine skills, stack movements and suggest patterns for center floor, across the floor and choreography. Add arm, hand and head movements to make the presentation more full-bodied. Note the "three and a break" combos.

Ball Changes (BC)

+Step:

★**SOFT SHOE TIME STEP:** 2 short and 1 long front essence

★**FRONT ESSENCE:**

```
1    a2   3    a4
st   BC   st   BC    SHORT ESSENCE - first two ball changes cross front
R    LR   L    RL
```

```
5    a6   a7   a8
st   BC   BC   BC    LONG ESSENCE - last three ball changes are done front, side, front
R    LR   LR   LR
```

BACK ESSENCE is taught in Level IV, when the brush and the spank are added.

Brushes/Spanks (br) (sp)

This exercise can be introduced at the barre and then brought to center floor to integrate into choreography.

+Heel Drops:
Start and end in Ready position. Progress through the following rhythms and REVERSE:

```
1 (2)  3 (4)  5 (6) 7 (8)
1      2      3     4
1      &      2     &
1      2      &     3 (4)
br     hdrp   sp    hdrp
R      L      R     L
```

```
a    1      a    2 (3) a4 5 a6 a7  (8)
br   hdrp sp   hdrp  BC st sh BC   RELEASE  REVERSE and REPEAT  3x in all
R    L    R    L     RL R L LR  L
BREAK:
8    1   a2 a3 4 (5) a6 7  8
st   st  sh BC st    BC br hdrp
L    R   L  LR L     RL R  L
```

Cramp Rolls (CRRL)

```
1&a2   3 4  a5 a6  a7 8
CRRL   st st sh BC  sh st  REVERSE
RLRL   R L  R  RL   R  R
```

Flaps (fl)

ATF: Develop clarity to master 3 consecutive flaps [a1 a2 a3 (4)]

+Ball Change:
```
a1  2   a3  a4 a5  6   a7  a8
fl  st  fl  BC fl  st  fl  BC  - VARSITY DRAG, traveling side to side or ATF
R   L   R   LR L   R   L   RL
```

+Heel Drop: Single and double heel drops can be added.

```
        a1  2    a3  4      a5 6 a7 8
ATF:    fl  hdrp fl  hdrp   REPEAT
        R   R    L   L
```

```
a1  2    a3  a   4   5  a6 a7  8
fl  hdrp fl  hdrp tip st sh BC st  3x
R   R    L   L    R  R  L  LR  L
BREAK:
(1) a2 3 a4  a5 6  a7 a8
    BC st sh BC st sh BC - WALTZ CLOG
    RL R L  LR L R  RL
```

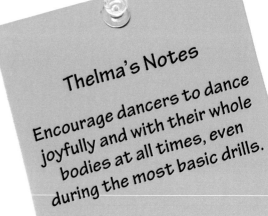

Thelma's Notes

Encourage dancers to dance joyfully and with their whole bodies at all times, even during the most basic drills.

Scuffs (sc)

+Leaps:
```
1    2  3    4  5   &  (6) &  7  8
leap sc leap sc leap tip    leap tip st  REVERSE and REPEAT 3x in all
R    L  L    R  R   L      L    R  R
BREAK:
1    &(2) &   3  4    &(5) &  6  7  8
leap tip  leap tip leap tip  leap tip leap sc
L    R    R   L  L    R      R  L  L  R
```

Shuffles (sh)

+Ball Changes:
```
1   a2 a3 a4   a5 a6 a7    8
st  sh BC BC   sh BC BC    st  REPEAT or clap on count 8 to REVERSE
R L  LR LR  L   LR LR  L
```

```
BREAK:
a1 a2 3   a4 a5 6  a7 a8
sh BC st  sh BC st  sh BC
R  RL R  L  LR L  R  RL
```

+Hops:
```
a1 a   2 3 a4 a   5 6  a7 a  8
sh hop st st  sh hop st st  sh hop st   REVERSE, traveling side to side with crossing shuffles
R  L   R L R L   R L R L   R
```

```
1  a2  a   3  4a5a6 7a8a1 2a3a4 5a6a7  8
st sh  hop st  5x in all                st  Do in circle then REVERSE
R L   R  L                             R
```

+Leap:
⭐ **MAXIE FORD:** step shuffle leap tip
```
1  a2 a   3  4  a5 a   6  7  8
st sh  leap tip st sh  leap tip st clap  REVERSE
R L  L   R  R L   L   R  R
```

Slaps (sl)

+Heel Drops:
This is a good opportunity to apply the "clock" concept for direction. Sarah Petronio uses the numbers on a clockface to help dancers direct their movements to certain places in relation to their bodies. In this combination, the slaps could be directed to the "3," then the "12," then the "9," ending the phrase facing the back and then reversing to the "3," the "6" and the "9" to face front.

```
a1  2    a3 4    a5 6    7    8
sl  hdrp sl hdrp sl  hdrp tdig hdrp  REVERSE and REPEAT both sides
R   L    R  L    R   L    R    R
```

```
a1  a    2   3   a   4    a5 a    6   7   8
sl  hdrp hdrp tdig hdrp hdrp sl  hdrp hdrp tdig hdrp  REVERSE and break down to 4 cts.
R   R    L   R   R   L    R   R   L   R   R
Out          In           Out          In
```

Stamps (STA)

+Steps:
This is an opportunity to accent a sound. In this combo, accent the counts "1" and "5."

1 2 3 4 **5** 6 7 (8)
STA st st st **STA** st st   REVERSE, facing side to side as in choo-choo
R L R L **R** L R

Stomps (STO)

+Ball Changes:
The toe drops in this combo do not transfer weight.

1   2   3   a4
STO tdrp tdrp BC 3x
R   R   R   RL

BREAK:
a5 6   7   a8
BC st tip BC
RL R   L   LR

REVERSE ALL ABOVE

+Hop:
This exercise helps to introduce the time steps that are taught in Level IV:

8   1   2   3   4   5   6 a7
STO hop st st STO hop st BC REVERSE
R   L   R L R   L   R LR

Steps

+Heel Drops:
This phrase can easily be moved from side to side with the steps coming in front, in back or alternating, as in a grapevine pattern. Add an upper body rotation and bring the rhythm into the hands and head to add style and dynamic energy.

1   2   3   &   4   5   6   &   7   8
st hdrp st hdrp st hdrp st hdrp st hdrp REVERSE
R   R   L   L   R   R   L   L   R   R

> **Thelma's Notes**
>
> Turn dancers away from the mirror, and resist keeping them in lines all the time.

CHOREOGRAPHY IDEAS

Tap Routine - "Smile" (Unsung Musicals). Note the uneven phrasing.

STEP ONE: SLAP, one arm up and one down, turning corner to corner.
```
a1   2    3    4      a5 6 7 8
sl   hdrp tdig hdrp   REVERSE
R    L    R    R
```

```
a1   2    a3   4      a5   6    7    8
sl   hdrp sl   hdrp   sl   hdrp tdig hdrp
R    L    R    L      R    L    R    R
REVERSE ALL
```

STEP TWO: STEP HEEL, 4x traveling R L R L, side to side, crossing second step.
```
1    2    3    4    5    6    (7) a8
st   hdrp st   hdrp st   hdrp wait BC  REVERSE
R    R    L    L    R    R         LR
```

STEP THREE: STEP TIP and CRAMP ROLL, 2x in all.
```
1    2  a3 4    5 6 a7 8
st   tip BC tip  REVERSE  Arms open.
R    L  LR L
```

```
1&a2 3    4      5&a6 7    8
CRRL st   st     CRRL st   st   (arms forward on CRRL and open for steps)
RLRL R    L      RLRL R    L
```

STEP FOUR: FLAP BALL CHANGE and BALL TAPS, changing lines, or moving upstage.
```
a1  a2 .... a8
fl   BC 4x, making a circle around yourself
facing front: 4 single tap-steps (R L R L) with opposing arms
fl   BC 4x, making a circle around yourself
```

STEP FIVE: SHIM SHAM VARIATION, traveling downstage to one line.
```
1    2    3    4    5    6    a7 8
st   tdig st   tdig st   tdig BC tdig  REVERSE
R    L    L    R    R    L    LR L
```

```
1    2    a3 4    5 6 a7 8
st   tdig BC tdig  REVERSE
R    L    LR L
```

STEP SIX: FANCY FEET! Hands go up on BC, first stomp is parallel with toe drops moving out, then in.
```
1    2    3    4    5    6    7    a8
STO  tdrp tdrp tdrp tdrp tdrp tdrp BC   3x
R    R    R    R    R    R    R    RL
```

BREAK:
```
1    2    3    a4
STO  tdrp tdrp BC   2x   (on last BC, turn to face stage R or L)
R    R    R    RL
```

STEP SEVEN: VARSITY DRAG, hands push up and out, facing another dancer.

a1	2	a3	a4
fl	st	fl	BC	REVERSE 6x in all
R	L	R	LR

a1	a2	a3a4a5a6a7a8a1a2a3a4a5a6a7a8
fl	BC	REVERSE 8x in all to make 2 lines
R	LR

STEP EIGHT: ROCK STEP, facing corner 2, then corner 1. Flap goes forward, first step is in place, then step back and last step is in place.

a1	2	3	4	a5	6	7	8
fl	st	st (back)	st	fl	st	st (back)	st
R	L	R	L	R	L	R	L

a1	2	3	4	5	a6	a7	a8
fl	hdrp	tip	st	st	sh	BC	BC	(move to corner 1 on step sh BC BC)
R	R	L	L	R	L	LR	LR

REVERSE ALL ABOVE TO CORNER 1.

BREAK:

a1	2	3	4	5	a6	a7	8
fl	hdrp	tip	st	st	sh	BC	st
R	R	L	L	R	L	LR	L

STEP NINE: SHUFFLE BALL CHANGES, traveling side to side, R L R L.

1	a2	a3	a4	a5	a6	a7	a8
st	sh	BC	BC	sh	BC	sh	BC	REVERSE and REPEAT 4x in all
R	L	LR	LR	L	LR	L	LR

Thelma's Notes

See the glossary on p. 188 for more information on stage directions.

STEP TEN: CANON, do this in 3 groups with diagonal arms on leap.

```
1     2    a3    a4
leap  st   sh    BC   6x
R     L    R     RL
```

Group 1 begins right away and does this 6x (24 cts.).
Group 2 holds 8 counts and does this 4x (16 cts.).
Group 3 holds 16 counts and does this 2x (8 cts.).

STEP ELEVEN: CIRCLE, make a circle around yourself. First to the R, then to the L.

```
1    a2   a    3        4a5a6 7a8a1 2a3a4 5a6a7 8
st   sh   hop  st       5x in all            st  REVERSE
R    L    R    LXFR                          R
```

STEP TWELVE: MAKE ONE LINE, moving downstage.

```
1    a2   a    3        4
st   sh        hop st        st  REVERSE and REPEAT, 8x in all
R    L         R   LXFR R
```

STEP THIRTEEN: REPEAT SHIM SHAM VARIATION, facing stage left (STEP FIVE).

```
1    2     3    4     5    6     a7  8
st   tdig  st   tdig  st   tdig  BC  tdig  REVERSE
R    L     L    R     R    L     LR  L
```

```
1    2     a3   4
st   tdig  BC   tdig  REVERSE
R    L     LR   L
```

STEP FOURTEEN: SHUFFLES, do as a canon, facing and starting stage L.

```
a1   a2   a3   a4
sh   sh   sh   BC   4x in all
R    R    R    RL
```

```
a1   a2
sh   BC   4x, all turn to face front
R    RL
```

March 4x, R L R L

```
1    2 3  4 5 6 7  a8
tap  st tap st tap st tap BC   REVERSE (tap can be replaced with a kick)
R    R L  L R R L  LR
```

```
1     2    (3)    4                    5
kick  st   pivot  st  to face stage R  st R for pose
R     RXFL L                          R
```
Big Finish!

STEP FIFTEEN: EXIT, flap BC off stage in single line.

IMPROVISATION ACTIVITIES

Music Recommendation

"Smooth" (Santana) - straight
"Mairzy Doats" (Maria Muldaur) - swing
"Take Me Out to the Ballgame" (Disney) - waltz

Goals

Dancers improvise with teacher direction for 4 bars (16 counts), starting and ending on time. Now that dancers are doubling their toe dig/heel drop combinations and have more control, encourage them to use just their toes and heels when improvising. Make sure dancers are all grooving while one dancer improvises. Teach them a simple 4-count rhythm [1 2 a3 (4)] and have them do it three times and freeze on the fourth 4-count phrase. Then have individual dancers improvise on the freeze.

LEVEL IV

AGES 9–11

(Dancers who have completed Level III)

STUDENT GOALS

Learn the following tap ideas: chugs, paddle and rolls, riffs, riffles, scuffles, spanks from the floor, single time steps, opposite heel drops, including pendulum and around-the-world cramp rolls.

Continue progression through the exercises detailed in the Rudiment Series, the Shuffle Series, the Slap and Flap Series and the Double Heel Series.

Begin to study the Spank Series and the Time Step Series.

Learn classic tap steps: Buffalo, Bombershay, Shim Sham.

Learn Soft Shoe Steps: Single, Double and Back Essence, Paddle Turn and Scissors Step.

Play eighth-note triplets and sixteenth notes and be able to distinguish between straight and swing rhythms.

Demonstrate full-bodied rhythm making during weekly lessons and while performing intricate choreography.

Improvise for 8 bars with confidence.

Demonstrate understanding of *Release*, *Relax* and *Ready*.

REVIEW

(INTRODUCED IN LEVEL III)

- BALL CHANGES IN ALL DIRECTIONS
- BRUSHES AND SPANKS AS INDIVIDUAL MOVEMENTS THAT CAN BE DIRECTED DIAGONALLY, TO THE SIDE AND TO THE BACK
- CRAMP ROLLS [a1a2] [1&a2] RIGHT AND LEFT
- FLAPS WITH BALL CHANGES, HEEL DROPS AND STEPS
- SCUFFS
- SHUFFLES WITH HOPS, LEAPS AND BALL CHANGES
- MAXIE FORD, IRISH, WALTZ CLOG, VARSITY DRAG
- SLAPS WITH UNDERNEATH HEEL DROP AND DOUBLE HEEL DROPS
- STOMPS
- STAMPS
- RUDIMENTS

MUSICAL RHYTHMS

FOR GAMES, IMPROVISATION AND CHOREOGRAPHY

Goals

Review swing rhythm [triplets = 1&a2&a3…]

Play running, straight eighth notes [1&2&3&4&…]

Introduce sixteenth notes [1e&a2e&a…]

Create rhythms with syncopated sounds, accenting the "&" and "a" counts

Find the "1" in standard swing, straight and waltz tunes

Sing the rhythm and participate in "Call and Response" activities

Distinguish between straight and swinging tunes

Play the following rhythms by clapping, drumming, tapping or using other body percussion. Post the rhythms on the wall or mirror. Dancers should be able to reproduce the rhythms accurately. Have dancers face away from the teacher. The teacher "plays" a rhythm and the dancers reproduce what they hear without concern as to what movements made the rhythm. Keep the rhythms short (4 counts) until the dancers become astute listeners and then extend the rhythms to 8 counts (2 bars). Have dancers use only their heels, or only brushes and spanks, to mimic the rhythm. Derick Grant calls this activity "no peeky peeky."

SWINGING RHYTHMS
1 2&a3 4 5a6&a7 8
a1a2a3 4&a5 6 7&a8
1&(a2&)a3 4 5&(a6&)a7&a8
1&a2(&)a3 4 (5) 6&a7(&)a8
a1 (&a2&) a3 (&a4) 5& (a6&) a7(&)a8

STRAIGHT RHYTHMS
1 2&3 4&5 6&7&8
1&2 3&4 5&6&7&8&
1&2&3&4& 5e&a6e&a7e&a8
1&2&3 4&5 6e&a7 &8
1e&a2 3e&a4 5e&a6 & 7 & 8

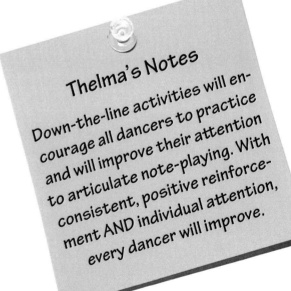

Thelma's Notes

Down-the-line activities will encourage all dancers to practice and will improve their attention to articulate note-playing. With consistent, positive reinforcement AND individual attention, every dancer will improve.

CLASS OUTLINE - LEVEL IV

The following class outline includes suggested tunes that will help teachers organize their weekly lessons. A brief description of what to do is provided. At this level, dancers will take their barre exercises to center floor and will supplement weekly review of basic skills with new challenges. As dancers learn new warm-up exercises, they will progress systematically through the curriculum. Read through The Next Step, where more details about skill development are discussed. Refer to Part Two (The Series) for specific exercises for each skill. See the lesson plan worksheet at the end of the manual.

Rudiments - center floor ➥See Rudiment Series (p. 87)
"Pink Panther" (Henry Mancini)
Dancers begin by walking around the classroom in quarter-note time, looking at each other, smiling, keeping the beat and moving independently of each other but sharing the same quarter-note rhythm. As they "hear" the end of the introduction, they randomly find a spot to dance. With R foot in *Ready* position, follow the toe dig, heel drop, toe drop exercises outlined in the Rudiment Series.

Cramp Rolls - center floor ➥See Double Heel Series (p. 105)
"Cantaloop" (Us 3)
Follow the progressions in the Double Heel Series. Reinforce the *Ready* position and *Release* concepts, and listen to each dancer individually in a "down the line" activity at least once during this series. To keep moving forward in the curriculum, do not skip any of the progressions. Keep track of your dancers' progress. For example, one week listen to each dancer's right cramp rolls. The next week, listen to left cramp rolls.

Paddle and Rolls - center floor ➥See Paddle and Roll Series (p. 147)
"Peter Gunn" (Donny and the Royales)
Follow the exercises as described in the P & R Series. Be watchful for the dancer who locks the knee or flexes/points the foot. The ankle and knee must stay relaxed.

Spanks - center floor ➥See Spank Series (p. 155)
"11 Long Years" (Us 3)
This introduces the spank that comes from the floor. Releasing the toe with the heel grounded is a new skill and should be taught slowly so that all dancers are using good technique. Do not let dancers lift the foot in order to spank. Adding this exercise in small progressions each week will yield positive results.

Shuffles - center floor ➥See Shuffle Series (p. 121)
"Tuxedo Junction" (The David Leonhardt Trio)
This sequence of exercises progresses quickly from individual quarter-note brushes and spanks to three swinging shuffles that cross, ending with shuffle hops forward and back and shuffle ball changes. As the year progresses, different tunes should be used to challenge the dancers to adjust to different tempos. Eventually, you will be able to introduce the hop before the shuffle.

Slaps and Flaps - across the floor ➥See Slap and Flap Series (p. 135)
"Birth of the Blues" (Oscar Peterson Trio)
As the year progresses, you might skip the double heel exercises done in duple time and do them with slaps and flaps in swing time. This is a good opportunity to reinforce the difference between straight and swinging rhythms.

Combos, Across-the-Floor (ATF) patterns and Center-Floor choreography
"That's Entertainment" ("Music for Tap Dancing," Kimbo)
Refer to the Combos section that follows for specific combinations to build new skills and reinforce the techniques introduced in the warm-up.

THE NEXT STEP

At this level, most of the fundamental movements have been introduced. The Next Step for these dancers is to strengthen and expand their vocabulary by combining ideas, moving from straight to swing rhythms, increasing tempo and incorporating more sophisticated upper-body rhythm making. The following basic skills are organized alphabetically. Included are suggestions for when and how to teach/expand these skills. For specific weekly exercises based on rhythmic progressions, **see Part Two for the Shuffle Series, Slap and Flap Series, Double Heel Series, Rudiment Series, Spank Series, Paddle and Roll Series and Time Step Series for Level IV dancers**.

Ball Changes (BC)

Ball Changes continue to be developed throughout the lessons. At this level, it's important to place the ball change to the front, back and side as well as directly under the dancer. In addition, challenge the dancer to combine a flat foot and ball tap for the ball-change rhythm.

Brushes/Spanks (br) (sp)

These continue to be practiced as separate movements at the beginning of the shuffle series. At this level, add the underneath heel drop, hop or step. Also, this is the level to add the spank that comes from the floor. See the Spank Series for detailed notes for teaching this new skill.

NEW TO LEVEL IV: The following are classic tap steps that incorporate the spank.

★**BACK ESSENCE:** spank step BC (step crosses back and BC opens to second position).

★**BOMBERSHAY:** progress rhythmically to ensure dancers are not kicking to release the spank.

1	2	3	4	5	6	7 (8)			REVERSE
1	&	2	&	3	&	4			REVERSE
1	&	a	2	&	a	3	&	a	4
st	sp	st	st	sp	st	st	sp	st	st - traveling to side - REVERSE
R	L	L	R	L		L	R	L	L	R

★**PADDLE AND ROLL:** also called "paradiddle" (heel dig, spank, step, heel drop).
See PADDLE and ROLL SERIES for detailed notes on teaching progressions.

1 & 2 & 3

Chugs - (ch) single heel drop as toe tap slides/pushes slightly forward

Be careful to distinguish between a chug and a heel drop. Once dancers learn chugs, they often want to do a chug in place of a heel drop. Use chugs selectively in combos and choreography, such as in STEP SEVEN in the Level IV tap routine.

Cramp Rolls (CRRL)

🐾 **See Double Heel Series (p. 105)**

Continue to emphasize clear articulations in various rhythms ([1&2&] [a1a2] [1&a2] [e&a1]) and add the opposite heel drop to change feet. This introduces the:

⭐ **AROUND THE WORLD Cramp Roll:** RLLR or LRRL

⭐ **PENDULUM Cramp Roll:** RLLR LRRL, with the legs swinging open and from side to side.

Flaps (fl)

🐾 **See Slap and Flap Series (p. 135)**

The goal at this level is to be able to do 8 flaps in succession in swing time [a1, a2, a3, a4... a8]
...with heel drops moving forward and side to side with alternating heel drops.
...with hops, steps, shuffles, ball changes to form various patterns and turns.

Hops - pushing off from one foot to the same foot

These skills can be drilled during the shuffle portion of the warm-up. Develop clarity and timing, as in:

⭐ **IRISH:** shuffle hop step in all directions

⭐ **DOUBLE IRISH:** shuffle hop step, shuffle ball change

Add the hop before the shuffle: Hop shuffle step, hop shuffle step... [1&a2 3&a4...]

Leaps - transferring weight from one foot to the other foot by pushing off into the air

Classic tap steps that have a leap include, at this level:

⭐ **BUFFALO:** leap shuffle leap

⭐ **MAXIE FORD:** step shuffle leap tip

Paddle and Roll

🐾 **See Paddle and Roll Series (p. 147)**

Before beginning paddle and rolls, be sure dancers are able to transfer weight clearly, *Releasing* the *Ready* foot with a *Relaxed* ankle on simple heel drops. Dancers also should be able to "play" the basic step/heel drop exercises in running eighth notes.

Riffs - begin by reviewing scuffs

2-sound riff: toe dig + scuff
3-sound open riff: toe dig scuff heel drop
                                  R   R   L
3-sound closed riff: toe dig scuff heel dig
                                  R   R   R
Practice in place at the barre for clarity; practice in quarter-note time before progressing.

Riffles - a 2-sound riff forward and a spank back (3-sound shuffle variation)

Scuffles - a scuff forward and a spank back (2-sound shuffle variation)

Shuffles (sh)

➤ **See Shuffle Series for progressions (p. 121)**
Shuffles become stronger and are done center floor in all directions: front, cross, side, back.
Combine with hops, steps, leaps, heel drops, tips and ball changes to create an endless variety
of rhythms and patterns.

Slaps (sl)

➤ **See Slap and Flap Series (p. 135)**
Slaps continue to be directed forward and side with double heel drops and opposite heel drops.

Stomps (STO)

Stomps lead to the development of time steps and other classic choreography. Be sure dancers
are placing the full foot down without weight. As the spank is developed, it combines with the
stomp for traditional time steps and the classic Shim Sham.

★ **SHIM SHAM:** stomp can be replaced by shuffle.

Step One: Do 3x, ending with a toe dig on the third count of 7.

8	&	1	2	&	3	4	&	5	&	6	&	7	
STO	sp	st	STO	sp	st	STO	sp	st	st	STO	sp	st	REVERSE and REPEAT on R
R	R	R	L		L	L	R	R	R	L	R		R R

BREAK:

8	1	2	3	&	(4)	&	5	6	7	
st	tip	st	hop	st		hop	st	st	st	(these last two steps can be jump out–in)
R	L	L	L	R		R	L	R	L	

Time Steps

➤ See Time Step Series (p. 167)
Dancers are now ready to learn traditional time steps, incorporating their mastery of hops, stomps,
shuffles, flaps and ball changes.

COMBOS

At this level, combinations will often include many different skills in one 32-count phrase. Thus, the following combinations are grouped around one main theme rather than two specific skills. These combos can be used for practice during center-floor work or for across-the-floor patterns. In many instances, you will note a traditional pattern of AABA or AAAB. The staging and upper body movements are not included in the text at this time. Teachers are encouraged to use these combinations in patterns that travel forward, back and side to side, or that are first done facing the front and then repeated facing the back, or that change lines or formations. Many of the following combos could work in a large circle or in small, individual circles. Likewise, when using these combos for choreography, dancers can work in pairs and take turns, as in a "Call and Response" format, or half the dancers can answer the other dancers. There is no limit to your creativity in using these ideas.

Ball Changes (BC) - move ball change out and in

```
1& (2) a3  &   a4  5  a6  a7a8
BC      BC br  BC  st sh  CRRL  REVERSE
RL      RL R   RL  R  L   LRLR
```

SOFT SHOE STEPS for Level IV dancers:

⭐ **SINGLE ESSENCE:**
```
1   &   a2
st  br  BC (crossing front)  REVERSE (Step can be replaced with a flap [a1 & a2].)
R   L   LR
```

⭐ **DOUBLE ESSENCE:**
```
1   &   a2  &   a3  &   a4
st  br  BC  sp  BC  br  BC  REVERSE (Step can be replaced with a flap.)
R   L   LR  L   LR  L   LR
```

⭐ **BACK ESSENCE:** add the spank once dancers are "pulling" from the floor.
```
a   1   a2
sp  st  BC (open to 2nd position on BC)  REVERSE
R   R   LR
```

⭐ **PADDLE TURN:** Use the numbers on the clockface (1, 5, 9 for instance) for placement of the first step of each ball change as dancers turn around the supporting leg.
```
a1  a2 a3 a4
fl  BC BC BC  REVERSE (The flap can be replaced with a single step.)
R   LR LR LR
```

⭐ **SCISSORS STEP:** moves from side to side with the ball change crossing front and the step and heel dig opening to the opposite sides.
```
a1  a   2
BC  st  hdig  REVERSE
RL  R   L
```

Brushes/Spanks (br) (sp)

Individual brushes and spanks are used in time steps, soft-shoe choreography and other classic tap steps. The following across-the-floor combo can be done in straight time rather than the swing notes indicated.

ATF:

```
a 1   a 2 a   3 a4 a 5   a 6 a   7 a8 a 1   a 2 a   3 a4 a5 a (6) a  7   (8)
br hop st br hop st BC br hop st br hop st BC br hop st br hop st BC BC st   sp hop   REVERSE
R  L    R L  R    L RL R  L    R L  R    L RL R  L    R L  R    L RL RL R    L  R
```

Cramp Rolls (CRRL)

The beginning of the following cramp-roll combination is part of Bill "Bojangles" Robinson's dance to "Doin' the New Lowdown." Note the pendulum cramp rolls in the BREAK.

```
8&a1 2 3    4 5 6    7          BREAK:
CRRL tip hdrp st tip hdrp st 3x  8&a1  2&a3  4&a5   6 7
LRLR L  R    L R  L   R          CRRL  CRRL  CRRL  st st
                                 LRRL  RLLR  LRRL  R  L
```

Flaps (fl)

👞 **See Slap and Flap Series for other ideas (p. 135)**

ATF:

```
a1 a2 a3 a4   a5 a6 a7  a8 a1 a2  a3 a4 a5  a6 a7 a8
fl fl fl BC   fl sh BC fl fl BC fl fl BC fl sh BC  REVERSE
R  L  R  LR   L  R  RL R  L  RL R  L  RL R  L  LR
```

Hops

👞 See Time Step Series for other ideas (p. 167)

```
1    &a 2 3 a4 a   5 a6 a7 8
hop sh st st sh hop st fl BC st  REVERSE traveling side to side
L    R  R L R  L    R L RL R
```

Leaps - note the accented note in the break

```
a1 2   a 3 4 5   a6 a7 8
fl  hdrp sp st st leap sh BC st   REVERSE and REPEAT 3x in all
R   R    L  L R L   R  RL R
```

BREAK: start on count 8 of the third set

```
8    a1 a2 3    a4 a5 a (6) a7
leap sh BC leap sh BC step BC
R    L  LR L    R  RL R    LR
```

Paddle and Rolls

See Paddle and Roll Series for teaching tips (p. 147)

```
1    &  2   &   3 (4) 5   & 6   &   7 (8)
hdig sp tdig hdrp st       hdig sp tdig hdrp st
R    R  R    R   L         R    R  R    R   L
```

```
1    &  2   &   3  4  5  & 6  &  7  (8)
hdig sp tdig hdrp st st hdig sp tdig hdrp STA   REVERSE all 16 cts.
R    R  R    R    L  R  L  L    L  R
```

Riffs - 3-sounds: tdig, scuff, hdrp

The open 3-sound riff ends with the foot *Released*, *Relaxed* and in front. This combo follows the A A B A pattern with the break on the third count of 8.

```
1  &a2 a  3  4  &a5 a  6  a7 a8
st riff   sp st st riff   sp st fl BC   REVERSE
R  LLR L  L  R  LLR L  L  R  LR
```

```
1  &a2 a  3  a4 5  &a6 a  7  a8
st riff   sp st BC st riff   sp st BC
R  LLR L  L  RL R  LLR L  L  RL
```

```
1  &a2 a  3  4  &a5 a  6  a7 a8
st riff   sp st st riff   sp st fl BC
R  LLR L  L  R  LLR L  L  R  LR
```

Shuffles - (sh) substitute a riffle or a scuffle when dancers are ready

See Shuffle Series for more ideas (p. 121)
The following variation of the waltz clog includes a leap.

```
1  a2 a3 4  a5 a6 a   7& a8
st sh BC st sh BC leap sh BC   REVERSE and REPEAT 3x
R  L  LR L  R  RL R    L  LR
```

BREAK:
```
a    1& a2 3  a    4& a5 6  a   7& a8
leap sh BC st leap sh BC st leap sh BC
L    R  RL R  L    R  RL R  L    R  RL
```

★**BUFFALO:** this often travels side to side with first "leap foot" coming to coupé in front of second "leap foot."
```
1    &a 2    3  &a 4    5  &a 6    a7 a8
leap sh leap leap sh leap leap sh leap fl  BC REVERSE
R    L  L    R    L  L    R    L  L    R  LR
```

64

Slaps (sl)

☛See Slap and Flap Series for more ideas (p. 135)

```
a1 2    a3 4    a5 a    6    7       8
sl hdrp sl  hdrp sl  hdrp hdrp st     st   REVERSE
R L   R  L   R  L   R     LXBR R
```

```
a1 a   2    3       4  a5 a   6    7       8
sl hdrp hdrp st      st  sl  hdrp hdrp st      st
R L   R   LXBR R  L   R    L     RXBL L
```

```
a1 2   (3)  a4  a5   a    (6)  a7  (8)
sl hdrp BC  sl  hdrp     BC      (note accent)
R L    RL  R   L        RL
```

CHOREOGRAPHY IDEAS

Tap Routine - *"Boogie Woogie Bugle Boy"* (Andrews Sisters), *edited for performance*

This tune is in 12-bar phrases, so note how the choreography coincides with the musical phrasing. There are many opportunities for complex staging.

INTRO: Wait 16 cts.
Entrance: fl BC 8x to upstage lines; fl BC 8x, traveling downstage.

STEP ONE: Corner step with "L" arms toward corners.

```
a1   2    a3   4    a5   6    a7    8
sl   hdrp sl   hdrp sl   hdrp sl    hdrp  (direct slaps in a compass turn to corners 1, 2, 3, 4)
R    L    R    L    R    L    R     L
```

```
a1  2    a    3 4 5    a6 a7 8
fl  hdrp sp   st st leap sh BC st   (face front)
R   R    L    L R L    R  RL R
REVERSE above 16 cts.
```

BREAK: Front row turns to face stage R; back row turns to face stage L.

```
a1  2    a    3 4
fl  hdrp sp   st st   REVERSE and REPEAT 4x in all
R   R    L    L R
```

STEP TWO: Travel downstage/upstage and stage R to L, ending in one row.

```
a1 a2 a    3 4 a5 a   6  a7 a8
fl  sh hop st st sh hop st fl  BC   REVERSE, traveling between downstage and upstage
R  L R   L R L R   L R LR
```

```
a1 a   2 3 a4 a5   a6   a7 a8
sh hop st st fl sh  BC  fl   BC 2x, traveling stage R to L or from stage L to R with half turn on hop
R  L   R L R L   LR  L  RL
```

```
a1 a2 a    3 4 a5 a   6  a7 a8
fl  sh  hop st st  sh  hop st fl BC   (travel upstage or downstage as in first phrase)
R  L R   L R L   R   L R LR
```

```
a1 a2 a    3 4 5 6    7   (8)
fl  sh hop st st st  click jump (all dancers face front on click* jump, landing with feet open to 2nd)
L  R L   R L R
*click - Hit feet together, in this case in the air.
```

3 4 & a 5

STEP THREE: Back Essence (the BC on counts a2, a4 and a8 opens to 2nd position).

```
1    a2 3    a4 5 a   6& a7 a8
st   BC st   BC st leap sh BC BC  3x
RXBL LR LXBR RL R L    R   RL RL
```

BREAK:
```
(1)  a2 3 4 5  6    7    (8)
     BC st st br sp      tip
     RL R L R   RXF      RXF
```

```
a1 a   2 3 a4 a5 a6 a   7 8
sh hop st st fl BC sh hop st st  REVERSE
R  L   R L R    LR L  R    L R
```

STEP FOUR: Kick (K), with opposition "L" arms. This step travels front to back.
```
1 2 3 4 5 & (6) a7 8
K st st st st sc    BC lunge
R RL RL R     RL R
```

```
(1) 2 3 4 5& (6) a7 8
    st st st BC     BC st
    L R L RL     RL R
```

```
1    a2 a3 4 5 a6 a7 a8
leap sh BC st st fl fl   fl
L    R RL R L R L    R
```

```
a1 a2  a3 a4 a5  a6 a7 a8
BC fl  fl BC fl  fl BC fl
LR L   R  LR L   R  LR L
```

REPEAT Kick phrase ending in clump facing back or front.
```
1 2 3 4 5 & (6) a7 8
K st st st st sc    BC lunge
R RL RL R     RL R
```

Then all face front with:
```
(1) 2 3 4 (5) 6 7 8
    st st st    st st tdig
    L R L     R L R
```

Thelma's Notes

Incorporate head and arm movements to polish the routine.

STEP FIVE: Double heel drop and opposition heels, all moving together in clump.

```
1 a   2   3 a   4   5 a   6   7 a   8
st hdrp hdrp st hdrp hdrp st hdrp hdrp st hdrp hdrp  (out–in–out–in)
R  R    L   R   L   R    L   L    R   L   R    L
```

```
1 a   2   3 a   4   5 a   6   7 a   8
st hdrp hdrp st hdrp hdrp st hdrp hdrp st hdrp hdrp  (travel forward)
R  L    R   L   R   L    L   R    L   R   L    R    L
```

REPEAT all above, traveling backward on second part.

BREAK:
fl BC (7x with st or st st to "V" formation.) RELEASE R or L for next section.

STEP SIX: Varsity Drag side to side and forward/back with opposition arms.
Some dancers start traveling "in" and others move "out." Arms start either up or down and alternate throughout the pattern. Some dancers start R, some start L; weight shifts are only shown for R side.

```
a1 2 a3 a4 a5 6 a7 a8      a1 a2  a3 a4 a5 a6  a7 a8
fl st fl  BC fl  st fl BC     fl BC fl BC fl BC fl  BC  REPEAT
R  L  R   LR L   R  L  RL     R  LR L  RL R  LR L  RL
```

BREAK:
```
(1)  a2 3    4   a5  a6  a7  a8 a1  a2 a3  a4  5    6   7    (8)
     BC pivot st  fl  fl  fl  BC fl  fl fl  BC  pivot st  tdig
     RL R     L   R   L   R   LR L   R  L   RL  R    L   R
```

STEP SEVEN: Turn and sugarfoot: inside R turn with tip BC.
```
1 & a3 4 5    &   a7 8 (1) a2  3 4 (5)  6 7 8
st tip BC st chug chug BC st    BC sugarfoot sugarfoot 3x
R  L  LR L  L    L    L    RL R    LR  L R      L R  L
```

```
1 2 3 4 5 6 7        8
Sugarfoot toward stage R  tdig with salute
R L R L R L R        L
```

IMPROVISATION ACTIVITIES

Music Recommendation

"It's Only a Paper Moon" (George Shearing Trio) - slow swing
"It's Only a Paper Moon" (Ella Fitzgerald) - moderate swing
"I Wish" (Stevie Wonder) - straight
"Friends to the End" ("Toy Story") - soft shoe
"Take Me Out to the Ballgame" - waltz time

Goals

Improvise in a teacher-directed "jam" setting for 8 bars, starting and ending on time.

If the dancer has been improvising for a few years, then she/he is ready to dance for a full 8 bars with teacher support. With direction, dancers should be able to use only their heels, or stay on the balls of their feet, or combine two elements. One exercise would have dancers travel from one spot to another, given a specific amount of music. **Be sure to have dancers SING the rhythm while they are dancing.** Another exercise would have them use only their voices in improvising or only their hands as drum beaters. The more they build technique, the better they will become at playing clear, concise rhythms. Have dancers trade phrases with each other as if they are having a rhythmic conversation.

Thelma's Notes

Invite dancers to bring in music that they want to tap dance to.

LEVEL V

AGES 10–12

(Dancers who have completed Level IV)

STUDENT GOALS

Expand technique to include cross-over steps, hop before the shuffle, double and triple cramp rolls, pull backs, and four- and five-sound riffs.

Continue progressions through all of the series work, mastering the techniques and exercises included in each subject area.

Learn classic tap steps: Military Time Steps, Double and Triple Time Steps, Cincinnati and Double Cincinnati, and more Shim-Sham choreography.

Be able to identify the notes of a rhythm phrase and vocalize the rhythm through saying or scatting the counts.

Demonstrate improved listening skills, timing and ability to self-correct.

Improvise and perform choreography with confidence and individual style, integrating the full body into rhythm making.

Demonstrate the concept of *Release, Relax* and *Ready.*

REVIEW

(INTRODUCED IN LEVEL IV)

- SOFT-SHOE STEPS: FRONT AND BACK SINGLE AND DOUBLE ESSENCE, PADDLE TURN, SCISSORS STEP
- OPPOSITE HEEL DROP IN RUDIMENT EXERCISES AND IN CRAMP ROLLS
- PADDLE AND ROLL, 4 COUNT
- SINGLE TIME STEPS WITH A HALF BREAK

MUSICAL RHYTHMS

FOR GAMES, IMPROVISATION AND CHOREOGRAPHY

Goals

By this level, dancers should be able to identify quarter notes, eighth notes, eighth-note triplets and sixteenth notes and be able to express or "play" these notes with their feet, their hands and their voices:

1e&a2 &3 &4e&a5 &6 7&8   1 2e&a3 4&5 6e&a7 &8

As their listening skills are improving, dancers should be introduced to counterpoint. Some simple counterpoint rhythms are below. Before actually dancing the rhythms, have dancers sing, scat or play the notes with their voices or hands.

PRIMARY RHYTHM
1 (2) 3 (4) 5 (6) 7 (8)
1 2 (3 4) 5 6 (7 8)
1 2 3 (4 5 6) 7 (8)
1 2 3 4 5 6 7 8
1 (2) 3 4 (5) 6 7 (8)

COUNTER RHYTHM
(1) 2 (3) 4 (5) 6 (7) 8
(1 2) 3 4 (5 6) 7 8
(1 2 3) 4 5 6 (7) 8
(1)&(2)&(3)&(4)&(5)&(6)&(7)&(8)&
1a2 (3) a4 a5 (6) a7 8

CLASS OUTLINE - LEVEL V

The following class outline includes suggested tunes and warm-up activities that will help teachers organize their weekly lessons. By setting a specific routine of weekly exercises, dancers will progress systematically through the curriculum, reviewing and strengthening basic skills. New challenges are presented in an organized format. Read through The Next Step, where more details about new skills are discussed. Refer to Part Two (The Series), where rhythmic progressions and teaching tips are provided. See the lesson plan worksheet at the end of the manual.

Rudiments - center floor See Rudiment Series (p. 87)
"Sir Duke" (Stevie Wonder)
At this age (10–12), dancers can sometimes exhibit shyness and insecurity. It is more important than ever that the class begin with an activity that brings the dancers together in the common goal

72

of rhythm making. Have all dancers walk around the room "like a real person" in quarter-note time, insisting that they look at each other, walk with confidence, wear a smile, swing their arms and stay on the beat. Don't start the actual rudiment exercises until all dancers are joined in a commitment to the exercise. As the weeks progress, add interactive elements to the walk. Have dancers walk in half time or eighth-note time. Have them walk 4 counts and then improvise 4 counts. Dancers explore counterpoint by some walking half time while others walk in quarter notes. **With engaged students, the weekly progression of rudiments becomes exciting, challenging and meaningful.**

Cramp Rolls and more - center floor See Double Heel Series (p. 105)
"September" (Earth, Wind and Fire)
Emphasis is on clear note-playing and reinforcing the Released, Relaxed, Ready foot. Individual "down-the-line" demonstrations are critical to steady improvement.

Paddle and Roll - center floor See Paddle and Roll Series (p. 147)
"Downtown" (Shirley Scott)
Proceed slowly to ensure a relaxed ankle. Slow down if you see dancers flexing and pointing; dancers with stressed ankles will not be able to progress in tempo and complexity. Again, have dancers listen to each other and to themselves to ensure accurate note playing.

Spanks - center floor See Spank Series (p. 155)
"I Wish" (Stevie Wonder)
Line dancers up across the front of the room so that you can see each individual's technique. Progress through the activities as described in the Spank Series. Be sure dancers are not kicking out or presenting a heel dig before the spank. Spanks are crucial to developing good drawbacks, paddle and rolls and pull backs.

Shuffles - center floor See Shuffle Series (p. 121)
"Isn't She Lovely" (Stevie Wonder)
Up until now, dancers have been listening to straight tunes in the warm-up. Take a moment to have them identify the musical change. Begin the Shuffle Series as described, with strong, rhythmic brushes and spanks that are dynamic and precise, taking the opportunity when the movement is a simple quarter note to show the rhythm in the hands and head. With attention to shuffles in quarter-note time, dancers will be more able to increase the tempo and play swinging eighth-note triplets that move in all directions. Adding hops, heels and ball changes increases the aerobic benefits, improving strength and preparing dancers to maintain high energy throughout a performance. Military time step is introduced.

Slaps and Flaps - center and across the floor See Slap and Flap Series (p. 135)
"A Kiss to Build a Dream On" (Trio de Swing)
This tune is a nice, slow swing and will offer the opportunity to emphasize the Released, Relaxed, Ready foot that is crucial for good flaps and slaps. Insist that dancers demonstrate the lift before brushing and that weight shifts are clear. At this level, flaps will stay in place, contributing to good time steps. Follow the progressions in the Slap and Flap Series to add heel drops, hops and shuffles, expanding the complexity of cramp rolls, essences and other choreography.

Combos, Across-the-Floor (ATF) patterns and Center-Floor choreography
"A Shine on Your Shoes" (Tony Bennett)
Refer to the Combos section that follows for specific combinations to build new skills and reinforce the techniques introduced in the warm-up.

THE NEXT STEP

At this level, most of the fundamental movements have been introduced. The Next Step for these dancers is to strengthen and expand their vocabulary by combining ideas, moving from straight to swing rhythms, increasing tempo and incorporating more sophisticated upper-body rhythm making. The following basic skills are organized alphabetically. For specific weekly exercises based on rhythmic progressions, see Part Two for Level V dancers.

Ball Changes (BC)

By this level, ball changes are done in all directions and are combined with flaps, shuffles, hops, steps, spanks, brushes, tips, heel digs, toe digs, heel stands, etc. Be sure that dancers are staying on the ball of the foot unless you are specifically requesting a flat sound. Explore combining a ball sound with a flat sound and accenting one of the sounds.

Brushes/Spanks (br) (sp)

Now that the spank from the floor is being practiced in the Spank Series, the following classic steps can be taught and strengthened.

⭐ **DRAWBACK:** step spank heel drop [1&a] or [1&2] - see SPANK SERIES for progressions

⭐ **CINCINNATI:** spank heel drop shuffle step [a1&a2]

⭐ **DOUBLE CINCINNATI:** spank heel drop shuffle heel drop step [&a1&a2]

⭐ **PADDLE AND ROLL:** review 4 sounds. Move the "1" to heel drop, in quarter- and eighth-note time.

Cramp Rolls - (CRRL)

Review the alternate heel drop that leads to the Around the World Cramp Roll and Pendulum Cramp Roll. Also, have dancers stamp and cramp roll with a turn, as described in the Combos section.

⭐ **DOUBLE CRAMP ROLL:** add a flap into cramp roll [&1&a2]; [&a1&a]

⭐ **TRIPLE CRAMP ROLL:** add a shuffle into cramp roll [&a1&a2]

Flaps (fl)

🕭 **See Slap and Flap Series for more specifics (p. 135)**
The Next Step in flaps is to keep them in place, develop double time steps and lead into a cramp roll with a flap.

Hops - work on these during the Shuffle Series

At this level, the hop is added before and after the shuffle, which prepares the dancer for triple time steps. Make sure the hop is done on the ball of the foot and that the sound of the hop is clear.

Leaps - add "running" shuffles to the Shuffle Series

Dancers leap from foot to foot, as in: leap shuffle leap shuffle leap shuffle leap [1&a2&a3&a4].

Paddle and Rolls

See Paddle and Roll Series (p. 147)
In moving the "1" to the heel drop, look out for stressed ankles. Reinforce the Released, Relaxed, Ready foot. Be sure dancers are not locking knees on the heel dig.

Pull Backs - (pb) also known as Grab Offs (gr) or Pick Ups (pu)

Children love to learn pull backs!

Teaching Pull Backs:
Once the spank is developed, start with the double pull back, which essentially is spanking both feet at the same time with the landing on the balls of the feet, either at the same time or separately. As these develop, dancers can separate all 4 sounds of a double pull back. A popular way to teach double pull backs is to begin with two-foot hops.

⭐**DOUBLE PULL BACKS:**

| 1 | 2 | 3 | &4 | | 1 | &2 | 3 | &4 |

hop hop hop pull back and then decrease hops to: hop pull back hop pull back
To separate the sounds, stand on two feet, spank the R foot; before placing it down, spank the L foot, then land the R foot, then the L foot. [1& a 2].

⭐**SINGLE PULL BACK:** standing on one foot, pull back from one foot to same foot. Teach with alternating leaps: leap pull back leap pull back [1 a2 3 a4].

⭐**ONE-FOOT CHANGE/GRAB OFF:** stand on one foot, spank and land on other foot. This is often used in the Maxie Ford following the shuffle. See Combos for more details.

Riffs - add the 4- and 5-sound riff

These can be practiced at the barre so that dancers are able to focus on making the correct sounds without worrying about balance. See Combos for across-the-floor exercises.

Review 3-sound, open riff: toe dig, scuff, heel drop or closed riff: toe dig, scuff, heel dig.
4 sound: toe dig, scuff, heel dig, toe drop OR toe dig, scuff, heel drop, heel dig.
5 sound: toe dig, scuff, heel drop, heel dig, toe drop.

Shuffles (sh)

🥿 **See Shuffle Series for progressive rhythms (p. 121).** See Combos for patterns that combine shuffles with hops, leaps, steps, ball changes, flaps and more.

As shuffles increase in tempo and maintain clarity, the Military Time Step as well as the Triple Time Step are taught. 🥿 See Time Step Series (p. 167)

> ⭐ **MILITARY TIME STEP:**
>
> | e&a | 1 & 2 | e&a 3 & 4 | e&a | 5 e&a | 6 e&a | 7 & 8 | |
> |---|---|---|---|---|---|---|---|
> | sh hop st | st st | [REVERSE] | sh hop st | sh hop st | sh hop st | st st | REVERSE and REPEAT |
> | R L R | L R | L R L R | L | R L R | L R L | R L R | |

Slaps (sl)

At this level, the important skill is to connect to the floor without weight and recognize the difference between a slap and a flap.

Stamps (STA)

As dancers progress, they can be challenged to regulate the volume of the stamp so that it is not always loud. A stamp can be a flat foot with weight without being loud, as in the second step of the Shim Sham. This step also has a stomp (no weight) at the end:

> ⭐ **SHIM SHAM STEP TWO: PUSH AND CROSS** (heel drop can be replaced with a hop)
>
> | 8 | 1 2 | 3 4 5 | & (6) & | 7 | |
> |---|---|---|---|---|---|
> | STA st | STA st | st hdrp st | | hdrp st | REVERSE and REPEAT 3x in all |
> | R L | R | L R R | L | L R | |
>
> | 8 1 | & (2) & | 3 4 5 | & (6) & | 7 & 8 |
> |---|---|---|---|---|
> | st hdrp st | hdrp st | st hdrp st | hdrp st | st STO |
> | L L R | R | L R R | L | L R L R |

Stomps (STO)

As in the above choreography, stomps are integrated into many patterns that call for a strong stop without weight. The Next Step in developing the stomp is to strengthen the spank that follows it in traditional and rhythm time steps.

Time Steps

🥿 See Time Step Series (p. 167)

Toe Drops (tdrp)

As toe drops are strengthened in the Rudiment Series, they can be used more in choreography. Replacing a heel drop with a toe drop can add variety and fun challenges.

COMBOS

Here, as in Level IV, combinations will often include many different skills in one 32-count phrase. These combos can be used for practice during center-floor work or for across-the-floor patterns. In many instances, you will note a traditional pattern of AABA or AAAB. The staging and upper-body movements are not included in the text at this time. Teachers are encouraged to use these combinations in patterns that travel forward, back and side to side, or that are first done facing the front and then repeated facing the back, or that turn or change lines or formations. Many of the following combos could work in a large circle or in small, individual circles. Likewise, when using these combos for choreography, dancers can work in pairs and take turns, as in a "Call and Response" format, or half the dancers can answer the others. There is no limit to your creativity in using these ideas.

Ball Changes (BC)

This pattern combines elements of several soft-shoe steps: grapevine, paddle turn and front essence.

a1	2	a3	a4	a5	a6	a7	a8
fl	st	BC	BC	fl	BC	BC	BC
R	L	RL	RL	R	LR	LR	LR

[side back grapevine, flap into a paddle turn]

1	a2	3	a4	5	&a 6	&a 7	&a 8
st	BC	st	BC	st	fl st sh	hop sh	st
L	RL	R	LR	L	R L R	L	R R

[front essence]

REVERSE cts. 1–16

Brushes/Spanks

⬅ **See Spank Series for more ideas (p. 155)**
This is a good opportunity to teach Step Three of the Shim Sham:

⭐ **SHIM SHAM STEP THREE: TACK ANNIE** (toe digs have no weight)

a	1	2	a	3	4	a	5	6	a	7	a8
sp	tdig	st	sp	tdig	st	sp	tdig	st	sp	st	BC (open)
R	R	R	L	L	L	R	R	R	L	L	RL

Do 2x, then REPEAT through count 5, adding walk 6 7 (step into Shim Sham break)
R L

BREAK:

8	1	2	3	& (4) &	5	6	7
st	tip	st	hop	st hop	st	st	st	(these last two steps can be jump out–in)
R	L	L	L	R R	L	R	L

Thelma's Notes

Remember to read the rhythm out loud FIRST when decoding the combinations.

Cramp Rolls (CRRL)

🡒**See Double Heel Series (p. 105)**
Once dancers can do an Around the World cramp roll, they can turn during the cramp roll.

1	2&a3	4	5&a6	7	8	
STA	CRRL	STA	CRRL	st	st	REPEAT, ending on 7 to REVERSE
R	LRRL	R	LRRL	R	L	

Flaps (fl)

🡒**See Slap & Flap Series for other ideas (p. 135)**
This combo is a continuation of the previous BC combo that begins to introduce a soft-shoe time step.

1	&a	2	&a	3	&a	4	&a	5	&a	6	&a	7	&a	8	
st	fl	st	sh	hop	sh	st	fl	st	sh	hop	sh	st	fl	st	REVERSE
R	L	R	L	R	L	L	R	L	R	L	R	R	L	R	

Hops

🡒**See also Time Step Series (p. 167) and Shuffle Series (p. 121)**

1	&a	2	3	&a	4	5	&a	6	a7	a8	
hop	sh	st	hop	sh	st	hop	sh	st	fl	BC	3x
L	R	R	R	L	L	L	R	R	L	RL	

BREAK: note the accents

1	(2)	a	3	a	4	a	5	**a**	(6)	a	7	(8)
scuff	leap	tip	hdrp	st	sp	st	**scuff**	leap	tip			
R	R	L	R	L	R	R	**L**	L	R			

Leaps - note the leap in the previous break

The previous break could be developed into a new combination. This is a good opportunity to teach Step Four of the Shim Sham:

★**SHIM SHAM STEP FOUR:**
```
8    1   a2  a3  4    5   a6  a7
leap st  sh  BC  leap st  sh BC
R    L R  RL R   L   R  RL
BREAK:
8  1  2  3  & (4) &  5  6 7
st tip st hop st   hop st st st  (these last two steps can be jump out–in)
R  L  L  L  R    R  L  R L
REPEAT ALL OF ABOVE
```

Pull Backs (pb)

Note: A cramp roll can be substituted for a pull back in this phrase.
Now that dancers know the Shim Sham, teach the final break:

★**SHAVE AND A HAIRCUT:** There are many variations on this phrase. This one works well for dancers just learning pull backs.
```
8    1    2&a3      4    5   6              7
STA  STA  pull back STA  clap leap (AST kick) st
R    L    RLRL R         L          R    R
```

Riffs

Once dancers have practiced the 3-, 4- and 5-sound riffs at the barre, they are ready to travel across the floor. Here are two examples of traveling riff patterns. Combine the two for a challenge for your fast learners.

4-sound riff:
```
[ 1     &     2     &    ] 3  4 [ 5     &     6     &    ] 7 8
  tdig  scuff hdig  tdrp   st st  tdig  scuff hdig  tdrp   st st
  R     R     R     R    ] L  R [ L     L     L     L    ] R L
```
```
[ 1     &     2     &    ][ 3     &     4     &    ][ 5     &     6     &    ] 7 8
  tdig  scuff hdig  tdrp    tdig  scuff hdig  tdrp    tdig  scuff hdig  tdrp   st st
  R     R     R     R    ][ L     L     L     L    ][ R     R     R     R    ] L R
```

5-sound riff:
```
[ 1     &     2     &     3    ] & 4 [ &     5     &     6     &    ] 7 8
  tdig  scuff hdrp  hdig  tdrp   st st  tdig  scuff hdrp  hdig  tdrp   st st
  R     R     L     R     R    ] L  R [ L     L     R     L     L    ] R L
```
```
[ 1     &     2     &     3    ][ &     4     &     5     &    ][ 6     &     7     &     8    ]
  tdig  scuff hdrp  hdig  tdrp    tdig  scuff hdrp  hdig  tdrp    tdig  scuff hdrp  hdig  tdrp
  R     R     L     R     R    ][ L     L     R     L     L    ][ R     R     L     R     R    ]
```

Slaps - (sl) *this phrase can be straight or swinging*

&1	2	3	&	4	&	5	&	6	&	7	&	8
a1	a (2)	a	3		a	4	5	a	6	&	a	7	8

sl	hdrp	st	hdrp	hdrp	sp	st	hdrp	hdig	sp	tdig	hdrp	hdrp	REVERSE
R	L	R	R	L	R	R	R	L	L	L	L	R	

Shuffles (sh)

➳ See Shuffle Series for more ideas (p. 121)

Continue developing all the classic steps that include shuffles. At this level, dancers can expand on the Maxie Ford as indicated below:

Maxie Fords: (Alternating with a pull back/grab off)

1	a2	&	a	3	4	a5	&	a	6	7	(8)
st	sh	gr	leap	st	st	sh	gr	leap	st	st	REVERSE
R	L	R	L	R	L	R	L	R	L	R	

ATF: Introduce sixteenth-note shuffle hops in military rhythm:

e&a	1	2	e&	a	3	4	e&a	5	6	e&	a	7	&8
sh	hop	st	st	sh	hop	st	st	sh	hop	st	st	sh	hop st BC REVERSE
R	L	R	L	R	L	R	L	R	L	R	L	R	LR

Time Steps

➳ See Time Step Series (p. 167)

In addition to the traditional time steps discussed in The Next Step, dancers can be introduced to the:

⭐ **RHYTHM TIME STEP:** At this level, a very basic rhythm time step could be:

a	8	a	1	a	2a	3	a4	a	5	a6	a7
STA	STA	STA	STA	sp	st	STO	sp	st	STO	sp	hop fl	fl	3x
R	L	R	L	R	R	L	L	L	R	R	L	R	L

BREAK:

a	8	&	a	1		2	(3)	a4	5		&	(6)	a7	(8)
st	st	st	st	STA	clap	BC	STA	clap		BC				
R	L	R	L	R		LR	L			RL				

Toe Drops - (tdrp) *add toe drops into a crawl combination*

a1	a	2	a	3	4		a5	a6	a7	8
BC	hdrp	hdrp	tdrp	tdrp	STA	REVERSE				
RL	R	L	R	L	R					

1	&	a	2	3	4	&	a	5	6	7	&	a	8
tdig	hdrp	hdrp	tdrp	st	tdig	hdrp	hdrp	tdrp	st	tdig	hdrp	hdrp	tdrp
R	R	L	R	L	R	R	L	R	L	R	R	L	R

REVERSE cts. 1–16

CHOREOGRAPHY IDEAS

Tap Routine - *"Crazy Rhythm" (Harry James), edited for performance*

INTRO: Wait 4, 8 or 12 cts. Flap BC to 3 lines.

STEP ONE: DOUBLE HEELS with opposition arms traveling forward on cross. Add spanks when dancers are ready.

```
1 a   2   3 a   4   5 a   6   7 a   8
st hdrp hdrp  st hdrp hdrp st hdrp hdrp st hdrp  hdrp
R R   L   R L   R   L L   R   L R   L
Out       Cross       Out       Cross
```

```
1 a   2   3 a   4   5 a   6   7 a   8
st hdrp hdrp, st hdrp hdrp st hdrp hdrp st hdrp  hdrp
R R   L   R R   L   R R   L   R L   R
Out       In       Out       Cross
REVERSE all above
```

STEP TWO: SCUFF HOP, traveling side to side.

```
1   2   a     3 4 a5 (6) a7 a8
sc hop sp    st st fl    BC BC
R   L   R    R L R     LR LR
```

```
a1 a2  3 a4   a5 6  a7 a8
sh BC st sh  BC st sh BC   (sh and BC cross FRONT; step opens to side)
L  LR L R   RL R L LR
REVERSE all above
```

STEP THREE: DRAWBACKS, note accents and straight rhythm.

```
1  &  2   & 3  &  4 &  5  **&** (6) &  7  8
st sp hdrp st sp hdrp st sp hdrp **tip** hdrp sugarfoot
R  L  R   L R  L   R L  R   **L**  R   L R
```

```
1  &  2   **&**(3) &  4 &  5  **&** (6) &  7  8
st sp hdrp **tip** hdrp st sp hdrp **tip** hdrp sugarfoot
L  R  L   **R** L  R L  R   **L**  R   L R
REVERSE all above
```

STEP FOUR: SHUFFLE HOP, direct flap to corner 2 then REVERSE to corner 1 on cts. 7–8.

```
a1 2 a  3 4 a5 a  6    7 8
fl st sp st st sh hop step  st st REVERSE
R  L R  R L R L   RXF  L R
```

```
a1 2 a  3 4 a5 [a  6 7 a8 a  1 2 a3 a  4 5 a6 a  7 8]
fl st sp st st sh | hop st st sh hop st st sh hop st st sh hop st st
R  L R  R L R  | L  R L R L  R L R L  R L R L  R L R L
              counterclockwise circle
```

81

STEP FIVE: MOVE, dancers criss-cross, traveling upstage to form one line.

a1	2	a	3	4	a5	a6	a7	a8...	(a1	a2	a3	a4...	a8	a1...	a8)
fl	st	sp	st	st	fl	BC	fl	BC...	(fl	BC	fl	BC...			BC)
R	L	R	R	L	R	LR	L	RL...	(R	LR	L	RL...			RL)

BREAK: Swing arms and heads in opposition as flaps and spanks rock forward and back.

a1	2	a	3	4	a5	6	a	7	8
fl	st	sp	st	st	fl	st	sp	st	st
R	L	R	R	L	R	L	R	R	L

STEP SIX: TURNS (Maxie Ford), dancers alternate "turn" and "walk" phrases below:

	1	a2	a		3	4	a5	a		6	7	8
TURN:	st	sh	leap	tip	st	sh	leap	tip	st	st		(turn both Maxie Fords or just one)
	R	L	L		R	R	L	L	R	R	L	

	1	(2)	3	(4)	5	(6)	7	8
WALK:	st		st		st		st	STO (swinging walks up/down back to line or around self in circle)
	R		L		R		L	R

All end with R foot in stomp position in front on ct. 8.

STEP SEVEN: SINGLE TIME STEP

1		2	a3	a	4	
hop	st	fl		st	STO	REVERSE 7x in all
L		R	L	R	L	

BREAK:

5	&	(6)	a	7	8
hop	st			hop	st	st
R	L			L	RL

STEP EIGHT: SMALL CIRCLES, divide dancers into 2 or 3 groupings for circles.

a1	a2	a3	a	4	5	6		7	8
fl	BC	sh	hop	st	[st	Xback	st	Xfront]	REPEAT 4x
R	LR	L	R	LXF	R	L		R	L
					[	grapevine		]	

82

STEP NINE: Dancers continue movement and blend into one large circle.

```
a1  a2 a3 a   4  a5 a6 a7 a   8  a1  a2 a3 a   4    5  6      7 8
fl    BC sh hop st fl   BC sh hop st fl   BC sh hop st   st Xback st Xfront
R   LR L  R   L  R   LR L   R   L  R   LR L  R   L   R L      R L
```

REPEAT cts. 1–12 and then replace grapevine with flap BC out of circle to new formation.

STEP TEN: REPEAT STEP TWO: SCUFF HOP.

STEP ELEVEN: Maxie Ford in canons every 8 counts in 4 groups. All turn on last Maxie Ford.

```
1 a2 a   3 4 a5 a   6 7 8
st sh leap tip st sh leap tip st st   4x
R  L  L     R R L L     R  R L
```

BIG ENDING:

```
1       3     5             7
st  back, st  front, hands and head in, open to "L" arms and head up
R       L
```

IMPROVISATION ACTIVITIES

Music Recommendations

"Straighten Up and Fly Right" (Natalie Cole) - swing
"Bad" (Michael Jackson) - straight
"Let's Go Fly a Kite" ("Mary Poppins" soundtrack) - waltz time

Goals

Improvise in a teacher-directed "jam" setting for 8 bars, starting and ending on time.
If the dancer has been improvising for a few years, then she/he is ready to dance for a full 8 bars with teacher support. With direction, dancers should be able to use only their heels, or stay on the balls of their feet, or combine two elements. One exercise would have dancers travel from one spot to another, given a specific amount of music. **Be sure to have dancers SING the rhythm while they are dancing.** Another exercise would have them use only their voices in improvising or only their hands as drum beaters. The more they build technique, the better they will become at playing clear, concise rhythms. Have dancers trade phrases with each other as if they are having a rhythmic conversation.

In Level V, challenge dancers to do some "improvography," simple grooves they can use when needed. Have them create their own patterns. It's important to continue to discuss musical forms and phrases so their listening skills become finely developed. Using music of their own choice will inspire them.

PART TWO: SERIES

The
RUDIMENT
SERIES

I was introduced to the Condos Rudiments by many of my teachers, who studied with Steve Condos at the Colorado Dance Festival and elsewhere. His experiences as a street dancer and vaudeville performer led him to develop specific exercises to build speed and precision in small footwork patterns. His Rudiments have become a key element in tap study for all levels and are a central part of tap warm-ups throughout the world. The Rudiments discussed in this series and throughout the manual are variations developed for children. There are many great YouTube videos that show Steve in action. Instructional videos are available for purchase by contacting Lorraine Condos at lorraicond17@yahoo.com.

LEVEL I - AGES 6 & 7

Goal: To train the dancer to do toe digs, heel drops and toe drops with articulation and in quarter-note time, promoting strength and control in performing small footwork.

Technique: From a Relaxed, raised foot with the knee lifted and the foot hanging in a front Ready position, dancers press the ball of the foot to the floor (toe dig), returning to Ready for repetitions and ending with the toe pressed to the floor once repetitions are complete. Then press the heel down, keeping the ball of the foot firmly in place and releasing the heel for repetitions. On the last repetition, the heel stays down and the toe is released for toe drops, ending with the toe tap down. Combine the heel drop and the toe drop in a rocking pattern (early crawl) and transfer weight on last repetition to reverse complete exercise. Ask dancers "What's next?" at the end of each repetition to help them learn to anticipate and plan ahead. **It's critical that dancers maintain a relaxed ankle during these movements, and that the supporting leg be strong, with the knee slightly bent. Be aware of the dancer who locks the knee.**

Music Recommendation:
"Never Smile at a Crocodile" ("Tap x Three," Statler)

STATIONARY RUDIMENT Series

 ONE

In Level I, stay in half-time until dancers have mastered the technique. By the mid-year mark, you may want to combine some half-time repetitions with quarter-note time, and by the end of the season, Level I dancers should be playing all quarter notes. Leave the last count 8 silent so that dancers can anticipate and plan for what part of the foot will be working next.

Footwork Pattern: Dancers begin with 7 repetitions of each of the movements below before changing feet.
R tdig 7x - say "*What's Next?*" Dancers say "*Heel!*"
R hdrp 7x - say "*What's Next?*" Dancers say "*Toe!*"
R tdrp 7x - say "*What's Next?*" Dancers say "*Rock!*"
R rock from hdrp to tdrp 7x On last R heel drop, shift weight fully, lift L foot (say "*Change feet!*")
REPEAT all on L.

Progress rhythmically as indicated below.

Break down the repetitions musically:
1. Half time: 1 (2) 3 (4) 5 (6) 7 (8) 1 (2) 3 (4) 5 (6 7 8)
2. Combination: 1 (2) 3 4 5 (6) 7 8 1 (2) 3 4 5 (6 7 8)
3. Quarter-note time: 1 2 3 4 5 6 7 (8)
Reduce the repetitions to 4 counts and then 1 count of each.

TRAVELING RUDIMENT Series

👠 TWO

Once dancers learn to execute the toe dig and heel drop in place, they can begin to move across the floor, traveling forward and side to side. **Emphasize the initial lift of the knee/foot in order to get a strong press of the toe tap, with the action coming down, not reaching forward.** Some young dancers will only touch the top of the tap to the floor and won't bend the shoe to articulate the full tap and begin to transfer weight. Encourage small steps so that the dancer is pressing down and not forward. **NOTE:** Level I dancers will not fully transfer weight to one ball of the foot with a controlled heel drop; thus I use the word "*press*" to indicate the weight shift. The toe dig and heel drop eventually become "step heel drop" in Level II.

ACROSS THE FLOOR (ATF): traveling forward or side to side.

⟲ Say "*Lift   press   heel   lift   press heel*"   REPEAT
     (1)   2   3   (4) (5)   6   7   (8)
          tdig   hdrp   tdig   hdrp
     R   R   R   L   L   L

Add another heel drop to reinforce the quality of the sound and give young dancers time to begin to shift weight on counts 4 and 8.

⟲ Say "*Lift   press   heel   heel   lift   press   heel   heel*"   REPEAT
     (1)   2   3   4   (5)   6   7   8
          tdig   hdrp   hdrp   tdig   hdrp   hdrp
     R   R   R   R   L   L   L   L

⟲ Say   "*Press heel,   press heel….*"
     1   2   3   4
     tdig   hdrp   tdig   hdrp   REPEAT
     R   R   L   L

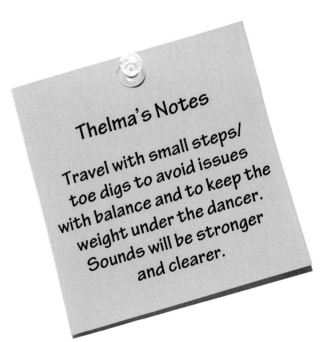

Thelma's Notes

Travel with small steps/ toe digs to avoid issues with balance and to keep the weight under the dancer. Sounds will be stronger and clearer.

LEVEL II - AGES 7 & 8

Goal: To gain strength and control in performing small footwork: toe digs, heel drops, toe drops. Begin with the stationary series in every class to reinforce the individual sounds. In the traveling series, the goal at this level is to shift weight fully on the toe dig, which becomes a step onto the ball of the foot with control over the timing of the following heel drop.

Technique:

From a *Relaxed*, raised foot with the knee lifted and the foot hanging in a front *Ready* position, dancers press the ball of the foot to the floor (toe dig), returning to *Ready* for repetitions and ending with the toe pressed to the floor once repetitions are complete. Then press the heel down, keeping the ball of the foot firmly in place and releasing the heel for repetitions. On the last repetition, the heel stays down and the toe is released for toe drops, ending with the toe tap down.Combine the heel drop and the toe drop in a rocking pattern (early crawl) and transfer weight on last repetition to reverse complete exercise. Ask dancers *"What's next?"* at the end of each repetition to help them learn to anticipate and plan ahead. **It's critical that dancers maintain a relaxed ankle during these movements, and that the supporting leg be strong, with the knee slightly bent. Be aware of the dancer who locks the knee.**

Music Recommendation:

"I've Got the Sun in the Morning" ("Tap for Kids," Statler)
"Oobabaloo" ("Happy Feet," Fred Penner)

STATIONARY RUDIMENT Series

During the first few weeks of Level II, review the breakdown of rhythms described in Level I. Once the technique of articulating the three separate sounds of toe dig, heel drop and toe drop are mastered at half-time and in quarter-note time, dancers are ready to progress rhythmically:

➤ **THREE** - *Release to Ready by shifting weight on last toe drop of rock.*

Quarter note: 1 2 3 4 5 6 7 8 (no wait on count 8)
8 of each on one foot: tdig, hdrp, tdrp, rock   REVERSE
4 of each on one foot   REVERSE
2 of each on one foot   REVERSE
1 of each = [tdig, hdrp, tdrp, hdrp] becomes a crawl as it moves slightly to the side

TRAVELING RUDIMENT Series

To get dancers to shift their weight fully to the ball/toe tap, it's important to demonstrate full-body shifts. Barbara Duffy calls this "UTA," or "Upper Thigh Activity." In the Jump Rhythm Technique®, this is called "sidedness." Emphasize the shift by lifting the whole leg off the floor, often in a very exaggerated style. Some dancers will understand this better if you hold their hands and mirror the leg action and weight shift you're looking for. **I always remind dancers that in technique lessons we exaggerate movements so that our bodies can learn new ways to do things. Once the muscles learn new things, we can make our movements smaller.**

➤ **FOUR** - *This first exercise is a very simplified version of a Condos Rudiment.*

ATF: emphasize the release of the alternate foot.

Traveling side to side: step open on R and close on L.
1 2   3 4   5 6   7 8   1 2   3 4   5 6   7   (8)
st hdrp st hdrp st hdrp st hdrp st hdrp st hdrp st hdrp tdig   RELEASE to REVERSE
R R   L L   R R   L L   R R   L L   R R   L

1 2   3 4   5 6   7   (8)
st hdrp st hdrp st hdrp tdig   RELEASE to REVERSE
R R   L L   R R   L

1 2   3   (4)   5 6 7 (8)
st hdrp tdig   RELEASE to REVERSE then REPEAT
R R   L   L L R

Traveling forward and/or back: Dancers begin by reviewing the basic toe dig (press) heel drop in Level I. Vary the following patterns and rhythms week to week to build accuracy and strength.

Level II Patterns: travel forward or back.

1 2   (3) 4 5   (6) 7 8
st hdrp   st hdrp   st hdrp   REVERSE
R R   L L   R R

1 2   3   (4) 5 6   7   (8) (shift weight fully for double heels on one foot)
st hdrp hdrp   st hdrp hdrp   REPEAT until weight shift is clear
R R   R   L L   L

1 2   3   4 5   6   7 8   (shift weight fully for double heels on one foot)
st hdrp hdrp st hdrp hdrp st hdrp   RELEASE to REVERSE
R R   R   L L   L   R R

LEVEL III - AGES 8 & 9

Goal: By Level III, dancers are able to articulate the toe dig, step, heel drop and toe drop with and without shifting weight and while playing simple quarter-note patterns. At this level, the goal is to play eighth notes accurately. This Rudiment Series overlaps with the Double Heel Series, which additionally focuses on cramp rolls, also double-timed at this level.

Technique: To accomplish articulate rhythm making, be sure that each dancer is mastering the movements and rhythms. Listen to one dancer at a time to ensure readiness before increasing tempo. Continue to reinforce the concept of the *Ready, Relaxed* foot, always reminding dancers to let the foot hang comfortably and loosely. Emphasize full-body weight shifts and the concept of Barbara Duffy's UTA (Upper Thigh Activity).

Music Recommendations:
"Peanut" (Maria Muldaur) - stationary and traveling
"Hugga Hugga" ("*Teddy Bear's Picnic*," Gary Rosen) - traveling

STATIONARY RUDIMENT Series

Level III continues the stationary exercises described in Levels I and II. Begin the exercise playing quarter notes, as in exercise THREE (Level II).

Quarter note: 1 2 3 4 5 6 7 8 (no wait on count 8)
Pattern: tdig, hdrp, tdrp, rock (8, 4, 2, then 1 of each, shifting clearly and efficiently)

🩰 FIVE

Introduce eighth notes. Notes for the toe dig are shown; repeat for the heel drop, the toe drop and the rock. Change feet by shifting weight on the last toe dig of rock.

```
1     2    3    4    5    &    6    7    &    8      1–8  1–8 1–8
tdig  tdig tdig tdig tdig tdig tdig tdig tdig tdig   /hdrp/tdrp/rock   REVERSE ALL
R     R    R    R    R    R    R    R    R    R
```

🩰 SIX

Continue to combine quarter and eighth notes, repeating sequence with rhythms:

```
1 2   3&4   5&6   7&8  (play rhythm with tdigs, then hdrps, then tdrps, then rock)
1&2   3&4   5&6   7&8  (play rhythm with tdigs, then hdrps, then tdrps, then rock)
REVERSE ALL
```
Change number of repetitions to 4 counts of each, then 2 of each. Finish with crawls.

TRAVELING RUDIMENT Series

After practicing the exercises above, move to simple step + heel drop patterns, in place and traveling forward, back and side to side. **Choose music wisely so that dancers can succeed in double time.**

🩰 SEVEN

Simple step heel drop patterns that introduce straight eighth notes: practice in place, shifting R to L on each step.

```
1 2   3 4   5 &   6 &   7 &   8
st hdrp st hdrp st hdrp st hdrp st hdrp tdig  REVERSE
R R   L L   R R   L L   R R   L
```

Practice in place and then move side to side
```
1 &   2 3   4 &   5 6   7 &   8
st hdrp st hdrp st hdrp st hdrp st hdrp tdig  REVERSE
R R   L L   R R   L L   R R   L
```

EIGHT

Continue introducing Condos Rudiments. Always begin with the first step heel drop rudiment (exercise FOUR). In Level III, practice this Condos Rudiment in straight eighth-note time, as well as in a swinging eighth-note triplet:

Traveling side to side: last toe dig is a touch to reverse.

```
1 a    2 a   3 a   4 a    5 a    6 a   7 a   8 - swing
1 &    2 &   3 &   4 &    5 &    6 &   7 &   8 - straight
st hdrp st hdrp st hdrp st hdrp st hdrp st hdrp st hdrp tdig   REVERSE
R R    L L   R R   L L    R R    L L   R R   L
```

```
1 a 2 a   3 a   4    5 a  6 a 7 a  8 - swing
1 & 2 &   3 &   4    5 &  6 & 7 &  8 - straight
st hdrp st hdrp st hdrp tdig   REVERSE
R R  L L   R R   L
```

```
1 a   2     3 a 4            5 a 6     7 a 8 - swing
1 &   2     3 & 4            5 & 6     7 & 8 - straight
st hdrp tdig   REVERSE and REPEAT 4x in all
R R   L
```

NINE

Teach the following Condos Rudiment, which adds a straight shuffle.

Traveling side to side:

```
1&2 &    3 &   4 &   5 &   6 &   7 &    8 &
sh st hdrp st hdrp st hdrp st hdrp st hdrp st  hdrp st  hdrp  REVERSE
R R R    L L   R R   L L   R R   L L    R R
```

```
1&2 &    3 &   4 &      5 & 6 & 7 & 8
sh st hdrp  st hdrp st hdrp    REVERSE
R R R    L L   R R
```

```
1&2 &     3 & 4 & 5 & 6 & 7 & 8 &
sh st hdrp    REVERSE and REPEAT 4x in all
R R R
```

Thelma's Notes

Don't forget to read the rhythm line first!

LEVEL IV - AGES 9-11

Goal: At this level, dancers are demonstrating relaxed ankles, knees and hips and are very comfortable with the toe dig, heel drop, toe drop and rock series, playing quarter notes and eighth notes and exhibiting good timing and clear sounds. The next challenge for them is to incorporate the opposite heel drop they are learning in the Double Heel Series into their opening rudiment exercise and to continue developing the Condos Rudiments. In addition, extend the rhythm into the dancers' hands and voices as they "hit" each note.

Technique: The *Relaxed* ankle remains a critical factor as dancers are progressing in tempo and complexity. Don't be reluctant to slow down and review the technique of *Releasing* with a *Relaxed* ankle. Note the opposite heel drop in the following stationary series. Refer to the Double Heel Series where opposite heels are also being introduced. When teaching opposite heel drops, have dancers press the toe dig into the floor and simultaneously release the opposite heel. As the heel drops, the toe dig releases.

Music Recommendation:
"Pink Panther" (Henry Mancini) - walk around the room and toe-heel rudiments
"Cantaloop" ("Hand on the Torch," Us 3) - more traveling rudiments

STATIONARY RUDIMENT Series

🥿 TEN - *Opposite heel drop*

Toe dig/heel drop/toe drop/rock variations:
It's still important to start in quarter-note time to ensure that ALL dancers are demonstrating good technique and shifting properly from one part of the foot to the other. Review exercises FIVE and SIX in Level III before adding the following variation, which includes the **opposite heel drop**. **NOTE HOW TO CHANGE FEET AT END!**

```
1    2    3    4    5    6    7    8
tdig hdrp tdig hdrp tdig hdrp tdig hdrp (keep R heel lifted after last hdrp, do not fully RELEASE R foot)
R    L    R    L    R    L    R    L
```

```
1    2    3    4    5    6    7    8
hdrp hdrp hdrp hdrp hdrp hdrp hdrp hdrp   (keep R hdrp down on ct. 7)
R    L    R    L    R    L    R    L
```

```
1    2    3    4    5    6    7    8
tdrp hdrp tdrp hdrp tdrp hdrp tdrp hdrp   RELEASE R heel on ct. 8
R    L    R    L    R    L    R    L
```

```
1    2    3    4    5    6    7    8
hdrp hdrp tdrp hdrp hdrp hdrp tdrp hdrp   RELEASE L foot on ct. 8
R    L    R    L    R    L    R    R
```

REVERSE all of above. Repeat pattern with 4 counts of each idea and then 2 counts of each idea. Once dancers are demonstrating good control and technique, repeat this exercise in the following progressively challenging rhythms, and again break down the pattern to 4 counts and, where possible, to 2 counts:

STRAIGHT	SWINGING
1 2 3 4 5&6&7&8&	1 2 3 4 5 a 6 a 7 a 8 a
1 2 3&4& 5 6 7&8&	1 2 3 a 4 a 5 6 7 a 8 a
1&2&3&4&5&6&7&8&	1 a 2 a 3 a 4 a 5 a 6 a 7 a 8 a

TRAVELING RUDIMENT Series

Continue reviewing the Level III exercises EIGHT and NINE, working in quarter- and eighth-note times and challenging dancers to move in eighth-note triplets and in sixteenth-note time. Progress steadily and add new concepts regularly, incorporating exercises from the Rudiment Series into the weekly warm-up.

🥿 ELEVEN

This is an extension of exercise SEVEN in Level III. Experiment with the placement of the quarter-note step-heel drop: **open to side and then close, or step together and then open.** Challenge dancers to do half and full turns, to cross the step and to swing.

```
1 2    3 a    4 a    5 6    7 a    8 a
1 2    3 &    4 &    5 6    7 &    8 &
st hdrp st hdrp st hdrp st hdrp st hdrp st hdrp   REPEAT with alternating placement of steps
R    R    L    L    R    R    L    L    R    R    L    L
```

TWELVE

In place and traveling forward and back, this exercise builds strength and control. Instructions are for eighth notes, but **start simple with straight quarter notes**. Make sure dancers are shifting weight fully on the step so that one foot is off the floor, *Relaxed* and *Ready*, while the other is working.

```
1 &   2   & 3   &   4 &      5 & 6 & 7 & 8 &
st hdrp hdrp st hdrp hdrp st hdrp   REVERSE and REPEAT for 32 counts in all.
R  R    R    L  L    L    R  R
```

THIRTEEN

This next exercise is one of the Condos Rudiments and is an extension of exercise NINE in Level III. It travels side to side:

```
1& 2 &   3 &    4& 5 &    6 &    7& 8 &
sh st hdrp st hdrp sh  st hdrp st hdrp sh st hdrp   REVERSE and REPEAT
R  R R   L L    R   R R   L L    R  R R
```

★ **CHALLENGE:**
In the Stationary Series exercise TEN, substitute a clap for the opposite heel drop. Combining clapping and tapping requires coordination and helps to build good timing.

LEVEL V - AGES 10–12

Goal: At this level, dancers are demonstrating a solid understanding of the basic rudiment exercises, including some of the traditional Condos Rudiments. As they continue to progress through the Double Heel and the Paddle and Roll Series particularly, they are being challenged to increase the tempo and complexity of duple rhythms. This Rudiment Series prepares the dancer by working on the small footwork that will lead to success in all areas of the tap curriculum. Although these are exercises, not choreography, have dancers engage the full body in accurate rhythm making.

Technique: The Relaxed ankle remains a critical factor as dancers are progressing in tempo and complexity. Don't be reluctant to slow down and review the technique of Releasing with a Relaxed ankle. Now that dancers have the technique of dropping the opposite heel, they are challenged to substitute the toe drop for some of the heel drops. **Dancers need to keep their weight over the arch so that either the heel or the toe can be used.** When possible, break down the patterns from two bars to one bar.

Music Recommendation:
"Sir Duke" (Stevie Wonder) - walk around the room and toe-heel rudiments
"September" (Earth, Wind & Fire) - more traveling rudiments

STATIONARY RUDIMENT Series

Continue to start in quarter notes to establish time and ensure good technique. Review the opposite heel drop in exercise TEN. Add the following when dancers are ready for a new challenge. **NOTE CHANGE-FEET PATTERN** at the end!

FOURTEEN

This is similar to exercise TEN but doubles up the toe dig, heel drop, toe drop and rock. Before "running" eighth notes as indicated, practice with a pause: 1&2 3&4 5&6 7&8

```
1    &    2    &    3    &    4    &    5    &    6    &    7    &    8
tdig tdig hdrp tdig tdig hdrp tdig tdig hdrp tdig tdig hdrp tdig tdig hdrp  (keep R heel Released)
R    R    L    R    R    L    R    R    L    R    R    L    R    R    L


1    &    2    &    3    &    4    &    5    &    6    &    7    &    8
hdrp hdrp hdrp hdrp hdrp hdrp hdrp hdrp hdrp hdrp hdrp hdrp hdrp hdrp hdrp  RELEASE R tdrp on 8
R    R    L    R    R    L    R    R    L    R    R    L    R    R    L


1    &    2    &    3    &    4    &    5    &    6    &    7    &    8
tdrp tdrp hdrp tdrp tdrp hdrp tdrp tdrp hdrp tdrp tdrp hdrp tdrp tdrp hdrp  RELEASE R hdrp on 8
R    R    L    R    R    L    R    R    L    R    R    L    R    R    L


1    &    2    &    3    &    4    &    5    &    6    &    7    &    8    &
hdrp hdrp hdrp tdrp tdrp hdrp hdrp hdrp hdrp tdrp tdrp hdrp hdrp hdrp tdrp hdrp RELEASE L to Ready on 8
R    R    L    R    R    L    R    R    L    R    R    L    R    L    R    R
```

REVERSE all of above.
Break down to 4 counts of each and then 2 counts.

Thelma's Notes

Use sticks or a hand drum for "Call and Response" exercises.

TRAVELING RUDIMENT Series

🩰 FIFTEEN - Introduce eighth-note triplets and sixteenth notes.

Dancers should be regularly playing quarter notes with their step-heel drop warm-up patterns and doubling up to eighth notes. At this level, dancers can be challenged to double up to sixteenth notes. In addition, they should be playing eighth-note triplets. They may not play all the notes accurately, but if you don't push them to develop speed and clear articulation, they won't progress in that area. With practice, dancers will begin to play triplets and sixteenth notes clearly.

TRIPLETS - when ready, dancers should play all triplets with no pauses.
```
1 &   a 2   3 &   a 4   5 &   a 6   & a   7 &   a 8
st hdrp st hdrp st hdrp st hdrp st hdrp st hdrp st hdrp st hdrp st hdrp   REVERSE
R R   L L   R R   L L   R R   L L   R R   L L   R R
```

SIXTEENTH NOTES - when ready, play all sixteenth notes with no pauses.
```
1 2   3 4   5 &   6 &   7 e   & a   8 e   & a
st hdrp st hdrp st hdrp st hdrp st hdrp st hdrp st hdrp   REPEAT
R R   L L   R R   L L   R R   L L   R R   L L
```

👞 SIXTEEN

This exercise is an extension of exercise TWELVE. After doing TWELVE, add this variation, which **substitutes a toe drop** for the second heel drop. Encourage dancers to shift all their weight to the action foot.

```
1 &   2   & 3   &   4 &
st hdrp tdrp st hdrp tdrp  st  hdrp  REVERSE and REPEAT
R R   R   L L   L   R R
```

👞 SEVENTEEN

This exercise develops the crawl, which was introduced in Level I. Dancers can first practice in place in quarter-note time. **When starting on R, travel moves to the L.** Be careful to shift weight fully to the last heel drop so that the other foot is *Released* and *Ready* to REVERSE.

```
1 & 2   &   3   &   4   &   5   &   6   &   7   &   8
st st hdrp hdrp tdrp tdrp hdrp hdrp tdrp tdrp hdrp hdrp tdrp tdrp hdrp  RELEASE to REVERSE
R L R   L   R   L   R   L   R   L   R   L   R   L   R
```

👞 EIGHTEEN

This is part of another of the Condos Rudiments, and it correlates with the riff that is being taught in Level V. A 5-count riff (5riff) is indicated, but you can adjust based on students' abilities. The 5riff is: toe dig, scuff, heel drop, heel dig, toe drop (no weight in this case).

```
1&2   &   3   &   4   &   5&6&7 (8)
sh tdig hdrp hdrp spank tdig hdrp 5riff        REVERSE and REPEAT
R R R   L   R   R   R   LLRLL
   OPEN       CLOSE
```

103

The
DOUBLE
HEEL
SERIES

The Double Heel Series is introduced in Level II. In Level I, dancers are focusing on executing clear and specific single-sound movements like toe digs, steps, heel digs, tips, brushes, spanks, taps and heel drops. To prepare for this series, dancers should focus on mastering the Level I Rudiment Series, which trains them to articulate the toe press followed by the heel drop. By Level II, their legs and feet are stronger, and they will be able to move into double heels. Note the Press Cramp Roll Series and the Cramp Roll Series are numbered independently. They can be taught simultaneously.

LEVEL II - AGES 7 & 8

Goal: To articulate the toe dig followed by two heel drops, shifting from one to the other with clarity; to step onto the ball of the foot and drop each heel rhythmically; and to experience the technique of Releasing either the heel or the foot to the Ready position with a Relaxed ankle.

Technique: Be sure to have dancers practice on both sides equally! Teachers need to be aware of dancers who lock their knees. Knees and ankles should be kept relaxed and the full toe tap connected with the floor. (Some young dancers may touch only the tip and not have the strength to really "press" into the floor.)

Music Recommendations:
"Oobabaloo" (Gary Rosen) - straight
"Consider Yourself" ("Oliver," Broadway original cast) - swing

DOUBLE HEEL - Press Cramp Roll Series

Progress rhythmically, ensuring good technique before advancing.

> **Teaching Press Cramp Rolls:** 3 sounds: toe dig, heel drop, heel drop. At center floor, start with a toe dig in place and then drop one heel, at the same time lifting the opposite heel, keeping the toe firmly connected to the floor. As the opposite heel lowers, release the entire foot to the *Ready* position. Once dancers have mastered the toe dig, heel drop, heel drop in place, move the toe dig to the side and move the pattern out and in, or in and out.

ONE - [1 2 3] ♩ "Pine-ap-ple"

Children benefit from saying the rhythm. One option is to use the word *"pineapple"* to indicate the three sounds of the press cramp roll and the word *"apple"* to indicate the two sounds of the toe dig, heel drop. Thank you to Jeannie Hill for this idea.

```
1   (2)  3   (4)  5     (6 7 8)
tdig     hdrp     hdrp (RELEASE R to ready position)  3x, say "Pine-ap-ple"
R        R        L
```

```
  1 (2) 3   (4 5 6 7 8)
♩ tdig  hdrp  Say, "Ap-ple"  RELEASE L on "-ple"  CHANGE FEET with release AST as heel drop
  R     R
```
REVERSE entire pattern above and practice until dancers demonstrate good technique of shifting weight, dropping heels, and *Releasing* to a *Relaxed* foot.

Progress rhythmically with the same pattern in exercise TWO; **move toe dig out and in**. Emphasize the *Release* of the *Ready* foot or heel throughout the exercise and especially when changing feet. Practice each rhythm until dancers are executing sounds clearly.

TWO - Move toe dig out and in or in then out.

```
1     2      3     (4)  3x  Change feet on counts  5    (6) 7    (8)
tdig  hdrp   hdrp                                  tdig     hdrp  RELEASE to REVERSE
R     R      L                                     R        R
```

THREE - Move toe dig out and in or in and out in straight and swing rhythms.

```
1    a    2    3    a    4    5    a    6    7    8   - swing
1    &    2    3    &    4    5    &    6    7    8   - straight
tdig hdrp hdrp tdig hdrp hdrp tdig hdrp hdrp tdig hdrp REVERSE
R    R    L    R    R    L    R    R    L    R    R
```

CHALLENGE: Add the slap that is also being taught at this time [a1a2....].

108

DOUBLE HEEL - Cramp Roll Series (CRRL)

Progress rhythmically, emphasizing clarity of sounds.

Teaching Cramp Rolls: 4 sounds: step, step, heel drop, heel drop. At center floor, work on strength to stay on the balls of the feet before dropping heels. Do not let dancers lock their knees as in a relevé. Although the action is to the balls, the dancer should not grow in height. Knees should remain soft, and the full toe tap should connect with the floor. Reinforce the double heel drop technique and *Release* as discussed in **Teaching Press Cramp Rolls**. The word "step" replaces "toe dig" because the weight is fully shifting to one foot. In this situation, the "step" is onto the ball of the foot. The heels come down separately and rhythmically.

ONE - [1 2 3 4] ♩ "Wa-ter-mel-on"

Emphasize stepping up onto the ball and dropping down onto the heels. A stamp or a step heel drop can be used to change feet. You may spend several weeks on each of the following rhythms before progressing. **PRACTICE ON BOTH SIDES! Be patient and make sure that dancers are completing all four sounds!**

```
1234                 5     (6 7 8)
CRRL  7x  Change feet on STA  RELEASE L  to REVERSE
RLRL                 R
```

TWO - [1&2&] ♩ "I want cookies"

Alternate quarter and eighth notes: choose music that can be doubled.

```
1234    5&6&    7&8&                 7
CRRL    CRRL    CRRL   4x  change feet on STA to RELEASE and REVERSE
RLRL    RLRL    RLRL                 R
```

THREE

```
1&2&   3&4&   5&6&   7 8
CRRL   CRRL   CRRL   st hdrp  RELEASE, RELAX, REVERSE
RLRL   RLRL   RLRL   R R
```

FOUR - [a1a2] ♩ "Vanilla cream"

Alternate quarter- and eighth-note triplets: use swing music.

```
1234    a5a6    a7a8                 7 8
CRRL    CRRL    CRRL  4x  change feet on st hdrp
RLRL    RLRL    RLRL                 R R
```

LEVEL III - AGES 8-9

Goal: To articulate the toe dig followed by two heel drops, shifting from one to the other with clarity; to step onto the ball of the foot and drop each heel rhythmically; to experience the technique of *Releasing* the foot to the *Ready* position of a *Relaxed* ankle. At this level, the goal is to combine cramp rolls with steps and press cramp rolls with slaps and shuffles. Additionally, dancers are challenged to move the double heel out and in and also forward and back.

Technique: Be sure to have dancers practice on both sides equally! Continue to work at the barre, combining double heels with slaps and shuffles. Teachers need to watch for dancers who lock their knees. Knees and ankles should be relaxed and the full toe tap connected with the floor. Some young dancers may touch only the tip, especially after the slap, and not have the strength to really "press" into the floor to deliver a strong heel drop. For additional exercises, see Shuffle Series and Slap and Flap Series.

Music Recommendations:
"Hugga-Hugga" (Gary Rosen) - straight
"I've Got No Strings" (Barbra Streisand) - swing

DOUBLE HEEL - *Press Cramp Roll Series*

Press Cramp Roll: The press cramp roll has three sounds: toe dig, heel drop, heel drop. Teachers should review the rhythms and exercises in Level II. Once mastered, add the following exercise to the series:

FOUR - *Rhythm notated is swinging; practice in straight time also.*

This next exercise moves the double heel out and in, or, as indicated, forward, back, to the side and then in to change feet.

```
1    a    2    3    a    4    5    a    6    7    8
tdig hdrp hdrp tdig hdrp hdrp tdig hdrp hdrp tdig hdrp    REVERSE
R    R    L    R    R    L    R    R    L    R    R
Front          Back           Side           In
```

CHALLENGE:
Add a slap [a1a2].
Move the above exercise in a half or full turn by placing the toe dig around the clockface.
    HALF-TURN: toe dig to the "3," "6," "9" and then in to change feet. REVERSE to "3," "12," "9."
    FULL-TURN: toe dig to the "3," "9," "3" and then in to change feet. REVERSE to "9," "3," "9."

DOUBLE HEEL - (CRRL) Cramp Roll Series

Cramp Roll: Four sounds: step, step, heel drop, heel drop
"*I want cookies*" [1&2&]
"*Vanilla bean*" [a1 a2]
"*Go to your room!*" [1&a2]
"*I like to eat*" [1 2 a3]
Review the exercises and rhythms in Level II before progressing to the rhythms below. Continue to use words or phrases with four syllables to reinforce the four sounds. Emphasize stepping up onto the balls and dropping down onto the heels. **PRACTICE ON BOTH SIDES! Be patient and make sure that dancers are completing all four sounds in the correct rhythm!** Add the following rhythms once the Level II exercises have been mastered. Use "Call and Response" so that dancers hear the correct rhythm and phrasing of the drills.

FIVE

Alternate quarter and eighth note triplets - REVERSE after break.
12a3   45a6   a7a8   "*I like to eat, I like to eat, mint chocolate.*"
CRRL CRRL CRRL 3x
RLRL RLRL RLRL

BREAK:
a1a2   a3a4   a5a6   7 8 "*Mint chocolate, mint chocolate, mint chocolate, all day.*"
CRRL CRRL CRRL st hdrp
RLRL RLRL RLRL R R

SIX

Introduce the "*Go to your room!*" rhythm: alternate "a." and "b."
a. 1 2 3&a4   5 6 7&a8 "*I said Go to your room! I said Go to your room!*"
    st st CRRL st st CRRL
    R L RLRL R L RLRL

b. 1&a2   3&a4   5&a6   a7a8 "*Go to your room*" 3x "*and clean it up!*"
    CRRL CRRL CRRL CRRL
    RLRL RLRL RLRL RLRL

CHALLENGE:
Have dancers make up their own words and phrases so that each syllable represents a sound.

a1 a2 a3

LEVEL IV - AGES 9–11

Goal: To shift weight by dropping opposite heels; to reinforce the muscle memory of *Releasing* the foot or the heel.

Technique: At center floor, practice the following to teach the technique of dropping the opposite heel.
Start in *Ready* position
Toe dig R in place
Release L heel
Drop L heel, then R heel
Release the entire *Relaxed* L foot to the *Ready* position

Music Recommendations:
"I Wish" (*Stevie Wonder*) - straight
"Paper Moon" (*Ella Fitzgerald*) - swing

DOUBLE HEEL - Press Cramp Roll Series

Review press cramp roll heel patterns in exercises ONE–FOUR. Note the strong duple "feel" in the following pattern.

FIVE - Note the placement, in or out.

Reverse pattern below, then break it down as shown, then add the FINAL BREAK.

```
1    &    2    3    &    4    5    &    6    &    7    &    8    &
tdig hdrp hdrp tdig hdrp hdrp tdig hdrp hdrp tdig hdrp hdrp tdig hdrp  REVERSE
R    R    L    R    R    L    R    R    L    R    R    L    R    R
Out            In             Out            Out            In
```

```
1    &    2    &    3    &    4    &    5    &    6    &    7    &    8    &
tdig hdrp hdrp tdig hdrp hdrp tdig hdrp tdig hdrp hdrp tdig hdrp hdrp tdig hdrp
R    R    L    R    R    L    R    R    L    L    R    L    L    R    L    L
Out            Out            In        Out            Out            In
```

FINAL BREAK: This pattern can be reversed, or you can reverse the whole exercise.

```
1    &    2    &    3    &    4    &    5    &    6    &    7    &    8
tdig hdrp hdrp tdig hdrp tdig hdrp hdrp tdig hdrp tdig hdrp hdrp tdig hdrp
R    R    L    R    R    L    L    R    L    L    R    R    L    R    R
Out            In        Out            In        Out            In
```

Teaching Opposite Heel Drops:

This next exercise coincides with the opposite heel drop in the Rudiment Series, Level IV. **By following the rhythmic progressions in different series, dancers are able to master new techniques and demonstrate them in different settings.**

SIX - Practice until opposition heel drops are understood.

Be sure to release after each heel drop.

```
1    2    3    4    5    6    7    (8)
tdig hdrp tdig hdrp tdig hdrp hdrp    RELEASE, RELAX, REVERSE
R    L    R    L    R    L    R       L
```

Break down, making sure dancers are releasing after second heel drop:

```
1    &    2    3    &    4    5    &    6    7    &    8
tdig hdrp hdrp tdig hdrp hdrp tdig hdrp hdrp tdig hdrp hdrp    REPEAT
R    L    R    L    R    L    R    L    R    L    R    L
```

SEVEN

The next exercise in the series is the same as exercise FOUR in the press cramp roll patterns, except that it has the opposite heel drop at the end to change feet. The notes given are for a swing rhythm, but the pattern could be done straight.

```
1    a    2    3    a    4    5    a    6    7    a    8
tdig hdrp hdrp tdig hdrp hdrp tdig hdrp hdrp tdig hdrp hdrp    REVERSE
R    R    L    R    R    L    R    R    L    R    L    R
Out            In             Out            In
```

```
1    a    2    3    a    4    5    a    6    7    a    8
tdig hdrp hdrp tdig hdrp hdrp tdig hdrp hdrp tdig hdrp hdrp
R    R    L    R    L    R    L    L    R    L    R    L
Out            In             Out            In
```

Travel forward or back:

```
1    a    2    3    a    4    5    a    6    7    a    8
tdig hdrp hdrp tdig hdrp hdrp tdig hdrp hdrp tdig hdrp hdrp
R    L    R    L    R    L    R    L    R    L    R    L
```

EIGHT

The next exercise is the opposite of exercise SEVEN. Dancers travel to the side with opposite heel drops and then change feet with same heel drops.

Traveling side to side:

```
1    a    2    3    a    4    5    a    6    7    a    8
tdig hdrp hdrp tdig hdrp hdrp tdig hdrp hdrp tdig hdrp hdrp    REVERSE
R    L    R    L    R    L    R    L    R    L    L    R
Out            In             Out            In
```

```
1    a    2    3    a    4    5    a    6    7    a    8
tdig hdrp hdrp tdig hdrp hdrp tdig hdrp hdrp tdig hdrp hdrp
R    L    R    L    L    R    L    R    L    R    R    L
Out            In             Out            In
```

Staying in place, shifting weight right to left:

```
1    a    2    3    a    4    5    a    6    7    a    8
tdig hdrp hdrp tdig hdrp hdrp tdig hdrp hdrp tdig hdrp hdrp
R    L    R    L    R    L    R    L    R    L    R    L
```

CHALLENGE:
Add slap when out and flap when traveling forward [a1 a2....].
Add spank when coming in and when traveling backward [a1a2a3a4].

DOUBLE HEEL - Cramp Roll Series

As with the press cramp roll exercises, it is now time to add the opposite heel drop to the cramp roll exercises. Another objective is to maintain the clarity of the four sounds while increasing tempo and "running" notes. A cramp roll that reverses the traditional order of heel drops is sometimes called an ★**AROUND THE WORLD Cramp Roll**.

SEVEN - "Around The World"

1&2& 3&4& 5&6& 7&8&
CRRL CRRL CRRL CRRL REVERSE, then break it down with next pattern.
RLRL RLRL RLRL RLLR

1&2& 3&4& 5&6& 7&8&
CRRL CRRL CRRL CRRL
RLRL RLLR LRLR LRRL

BREAK:
The final break for this exercise introduces the ★**PENDULUM Cramp Roll**, which swings from side to side, opening on the second step of the cramp roll.
1&2& 3&4& 5&6& 7&8&
CRRL CRRL CRRL CRRL
RLLR LRRL RLLR LRRL

EIGHT

The next exercise in this series is the same pattern as exercise SEVEN, but with swing rhythms [a1a2] and [1&a2]. Substitute these in the AROUND THE WORLD and PENDULUM exercises above. Use music that helps the students connect with the swing in contrast with the duple feel of exercise SEVEN.

CHALLENGE:
Swing the Pendulum Cramp Roll in a half-turn.
See Combos for challenging patterns that incorporate these opposite heel cramp rolls.
Add a flap before the cramp roll [a1&a2] or [&a1a2] or [&1&2&].
Change the rhythm of the cramp roll within the exercise, such as:

1&a2 a3a4 5&6& 7&a8
CRRL CRRL CRRL CRRL
RLRL RLLR LRLR LRRL

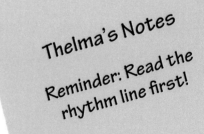

Thelma's Notes

Reminder: Read the rhythm line first!

LEVEL V - AGES 10–12

Goal: To *Release* and drop heels automatically based on what foot is needed next. Through practice exercises, dancers gain confidence and clarity in press cramp rolls, traditional cramp rolls and around-the-world and pendulum cramp rolls. In the Press Cramp Roll exercises, dancers are "running" their eighth notes and integrating a clap into the rhythm. Sixteenth notes are played in the Cramp Roll Series.

Technique: During rudiment warm-up, reinforce the opposite heel-drop exercise in center floor to prepare dancers for opposition heel work in this Double Heel Series. In addition, for cramp rolls, dancers need to push off so that both feet are in the air but are landing separately.

Music Recommendations:
"September" (Earth, Wind & Fire) - straight
"T'aint What You Do" (Ella Fitzgerald) - swing

DOUBLE HEEL - Press Cramp Roll Series

🥿 NINE

In this exercise, the toe dig can be done to the side, then to the front, back, side and then in, with opposite heels to change feet.

```
1    &    2    &    3    &    4    &    5    &    6    &    7    &    8
tdig hdrp hdrp tdig hdrp hdrp tdig hdrp hdrp tdig hdrp hdrp tdig hdrp hdrp   REVERSE
R    R    L    R    R    L    R    R    L    R    R    L    R    L    R
Side           Front          Back           Side           In
```

```
1    &    2    &    3    &    4    .... 5 & 6 & 7 & 8
tdig hdrp hdrp tdig hdrp hdrp clap
R    R    L    R    L    R       RELEASE L foot, then REVERSE
Side      In
```

Travel forward or back:
```
1    &    2    &    3    &    4    &    5    &    6    &    7    &    8
tdig hdrp hdrp tdig hdrp hdrp tdig hdrp hdrp tdig hdrp hdrp tdig hdrp hdrp
R    L    R    L    R    L    R    L    R    L    R    L    R    L    R
```

REVERSE all parts of this exercise.

DOUBLE HEEL - Cramp Roll Series

🥿 TEN

At this level, dancers are working in sixteenth-note time with the **Military Time Step** (exercise THIRTEEN in the Shuffle Series). The same rhythm can be "played" with cramp rolls. This next exercise requires careful attention to ensure that dancers are playing all the notes. Make sure they are pushing off to get both feet up and are landing separately.

```
e&a1 & 2  e&a3 & 4  e&a5  e&a6   e&a7 & 8
CRRL st st CRRL st st CRRL  CRRL  CRRL st st  REPEAT 3x
RLRL R L  RLRL R L  RLRL  RLRL  RLRL R L
```

BREAK:
```
e&a1 e&a2  e&a3  & 4  e&a5  e&a6  & 7  8
CRRL CRRL  CRRL  st st CRRL  CRRL  st st st  REVERSE ALL
RLRL RLRL  RLRL  R L  RLRL  RLRL  R L  R
```

⭐ CHALLENGE:
Add slaps, flaps, spanks and shuffles for variations to the above exercises.

The
SHUFFLE
SERIES

LEVEL I - AGES 6 & 7

Get Ready: LOOSE ANKLES - NO POINTING OR FLEXING! Emphasize proper barre etiquette and placement. Build strength and stamina in supporting leg by keeping weight over arch and hand forward to stack shoulder, hip, knee and ankle. The *Ready* position (working leg lifted, slightly bent with relaxed foot hanging loosely from knee) will be used throughout dancers' training, so continue to reinforce this concept regularly.

Goal: Brush + Spank as individual movements
Initially, have dancers brush the toe tap forward and back with big sweeping movements. I suggest they first imagine painting a stripe on the floor, using their hands and arms. As they master the ability to use just the toe tap and keep the heel off the floor, I introduce the idea of the *Ready* position. Encourage dancers to connect with the floor slightly in front of the supporting leg.

Technique: Brush down/forward with leg lengthening, but not locking, and ankle relaxed, with toes flat in shoe. Spank down/up to starting position, keeping ankle loose, *Relaxed* and *Ready*.

At the barre, in *Ready* **position:** Move sequentially through the series, doing as many repetitions as necessary. Always start with the simplest movement! Make sure dancers master the brush and the spank independently. Don't forget to practice on both sides equally.

Music Recommendations:
"Red Red Robin" ("Ready Set Dance," Statler)

ONE

The sequence of rhythms is noted below, with pauses in parentheses. **Do as many repetitions of each phrase as necessary**, changing when the majority of the class has mastered the idea. Each week, begin with the simplest phrase in order to increase strength, stamina and technique, and to promote relaxation in the movement. Always return to *Ready*.

a. Brush R spank R [1 (2 3 4) 5 (6   7 8)]   REPEAT
b. Brush R spank R [1 (2) 3 (4) 5 (6) 7 (8)]   REPEAT
c. Brush R spank R [1 2 (3 4) 5 6 (7 8)] *"shuf-fle"* REPEAT
d. Brush R spank R [1 2 3 4 (5 6 7 8)]   REPEAT
e. Brush R spank R [1 2 3 4 5 6 7 8]   *"let it swing"*

REVERSE ALL

TWO

Continuing at the barre: The barre enables dancers to stay on the balls of their feet while marching/stepping. I use the word "march" to encourage lifting the knee and stepping onto the ball of the foot while in place. **Eventually, this marching becomes less about the knee lifting and more about a light step onto the ball of the foot.** Be sure dancers are *Releasing* to a *Ready* position after each march/step. As with exercise ONE, do as many repetitions of each rhythm phrase as necessary. It will take time for dancers to stay on the balls of their feet and learn to "rest" their heels silently. Reinforce all *Release, Relax, Ready* concepts after each march.

+Step/March (which become ball changes in Level II):
Shuffle R [1 2] (wait 3 4) march [5 6] (wait 7 8)   REPEAT
Shuffle R [1 2] march [3 4] (wait 5 6 7 8) REPEAT
Shuffle R [1 2] march [3 4] shuffle R [5 6] march [7 8]
Shuffle R [1 2] shuffle R [3 4] march [5 6] (wait 7 8)
Shuffle shuffle shuffle R [1 2 3 4 5 6] march [7 8]
Turn at the barre to REVERSE.

Take exercise TWO to center floor when dancers are ready.

1 2 3 4 5

LEVEL II - AGES 7 & 8

Get Ready: Standing at the barre, review relaxed ankle, proper barre etiquette and the *Ready* position.

Goal: To increase tempo and clarity, and play eighth-note triplets [a1 (&) a2]. Always start with clear, articulate quarter note brushes and spanks. As dancers progress through levels, it will be very important that they don't automatically spank every time they brush out! Teach your dancers to send the foot out and leave it there to build strength and isolate the single sounds before combining them for shuffles.

Technique: Begin and end in *Ready* position with ankle relaxed, knee slightly bent with foot hanging loosely. Be sure dancers are brushing only the toe tap to the floor, and that the brush and spank are in front of the dancer.

Music Recommendations:
"Orange Colored Sky" ("Tap for Kids," Statler)

🩰 THREE

Always start at the barre, going through the exercise ONE sequence of brushes and spanks. In Level II, you won't have to do as many repetitions, but it's important that the dancer continue to recognize the brush and the spank as individual movements. Add the following rhythm phrases after the sequence in exercise ONE is completed. Progress slowly; dancers may not master the double, swinging shuffles until months into the season. Always return to Ready.

With left hand on the barre:
f. Shuffle R [1   2 3& (4   5   6   7   8)]   REPEAT
g. Shuffle R [1   2 3& (4) 5   6   7& (8)]   REPEAT
h. Shuffle R [1   2 a3 (4) 5   6   a7 (8)]   REPEAT
i. Shuffle R [a1 (2) a3 (4) a5 (6) a7 (8)]   REPEAT
j. Shuffle R [a1 a2 (3   4) a5 a6 (7   8)]   REPEAT

Change to R hand on the barre to REVERSE.

🩰 FOUR

It's important for dancers to take their shuffles to center floor to reinforce the barre exercises in the series. Make sure dancers are Releasing to the Ready position before each shuffle. These are just two simple ideas that combine the shuffle with a step and a ball change. See Shuffle Combos in Level II for more ideas.

+Steps:
a1 2 3 a4 5 6 a7 8
sh st st sh st st sh st   REVERSE
R R L R R L R R

+Ball Change:
1   2   a3   4   5   a6   a7 8   a8
br sp BC   br sp BC   sh st   REVERSE, or BC to REPEAT
R   R   RL   R   R   RL   R   R   RL

125

LEVEL III - AGES 8 & 9

Get Ready: Standing at the barre, discuss proper barre etiquette and the *Release, Relax, Ready* concept (leg lifted, slightly bent with relaxed foot hanging loosely from knee).

Goal: To expand the direction of the shuffle to a diagonal crossing and uncrossing; to add the hop after the shuffle and to increase tempo to three swinging shuffles with clarity. Classic choreography includes Waltz Clog, Maxie Ford, Shim Sham and Irish.

Technique: Discuss the rotation of the hip that allows the knee to open, preparing to cross and uncross the brush and spank of the shuffle. Continue to work in quarter-note time, building strength and control in the working leg so that the brush and spank stand independently, particularly as dancers begin to cross the shuffle. No locked knees; relaxed foot/ankle; knee lifted; outside arm open to side and joints stacked naturally. Watch for the child who "sickles" her/his foot! You may need to incorporate exercises to build strength in weak ankle muscles.

Music Recommendations:
"'A' You're Adorable" (John Lithgow)

FIVE

Repeat a.–j. of Level I and II Shuffle Series: complete each exercise in parallel **AND in diagonal position, crossing and uncrossing.** Depending on dancers' progress, you may want to do a series of four parallels and then four crosses for each of the phrases below, alternating with as many repetitions as necessary to ensure good technique. REPEAT all on left.

a. Brush R spank R [1 (2 3 4) 5 (6   7 8)]   REPEAT
b. Brush R spank R [1 (2) 3 (4) 5 (6) 7 (8)]   REPEAT
c. Brush R spank R [1 2 (3 4) 5 6 (7 8)] *"shuf-fle"* REPEAT
d. Brush R spank R [1 2 3 4 (5 6   7 8)]   REPEAT
e. Brush R spank R [1 2 3 4 5 6 7 8] *"let it swing"*
f. Shuffle R [1   2 3& (4   5   6   7   8)]   REPEAT
g. Shuffle R [1   2 3& (4) 5   6 7& (8)]   REPEAT
h. Shuffle R [1   2 a3 (4) 5   6   a7 (8)]   REPEAT
i. Shuffle R [a1 (2) a3 (4) a5 (6) a7 (8)]   REPEAT
j. Shuffle R [a1 a2 (3   4) a5 a6 (7   8)]   REPEAT

Add new progressions: open shuffles to side and reach to back.
k. Shuffle R [a1a2a3 (4)], waiting with foot crossed in front, uncrossing, finishing in *Ready*.
l. Continuous swinging shuffles: 4x, then 5x, then 6x, then 7x [a1a2a3a4…a7 8] step on count "8" to REVERSE

SIX

+Hops: in parallel at the barre. Be sure to practice on the left.
Hops are taught at the barre, with the hop being an extension of the spank. Like other concepts, begin in quarter-note time with pauses to assure that dancers are returning to a *Ready* position.

12   3   (4)
sh   hop   REPEAT many times to build strength and muscle memory
R   L

a1 2 (3 4)
sh hop   REPEAT many times to build strength and muscle memory
R   L

+Hops: center floor, begin by practicing in parallel, in place. As dancers progress, they travel forward and back with crossing shuffles and steps that open to 2nd position.

a1 a   2 3 4 a5 a   6 7 8
sh hop st st st sh hop st st st   REPEAT
R L   R L R L   R L R L

★**IRISH (shuffle hop step):** see Level III Combos and The Next Step.

ATF: Cross the shuffle, stepping front after hop.
1   a2 a   3 (4) 5 a6 a   7 (8)1 a2 a   3 4 a5 a   6 7 (8)
st sh hop st   st sh hop st   st sh hop st st sh hop st st   REVERSE
R L R   L   R L R   L   R L R   L R L R L R

SEVEN

+Ball Changes: It's very important to emphasize that the Ready foot needs to be off the floor in order to do a good shuffle. Start at a slow tempo in order to assure good technique. This is one example of a weekly shuffle ball change pattern for Level III.

```
a1 a2  a3 a4 a5 a6  a7 a    8 a1 a2  a3 a4 a5 a6  a7 a    8
sh BC sh BC sh BC sh hop st sh BC sh BC sh BC sh hop st   REPEAT
R  RL R  RL R  RL R  L      R L  LR L  LR L  LR L  L  R   L
```

Break down to 4 counts on each side.

EIGHT

+Leap: Leaps move from one foot to another; hops begin and end on the same foot. This pattern practices the last step of the Shim Sham as well as the Waltz Clog.

```
1    2  a3 a4  5    a6 a7 8  1     a2 a3 4     a5 a6 7 8
leap st  sh BC  leap sh BC st  leap sh  BC leap sh BC st clap   REVERSE
R    L  R  RL R  L  LR L  R    L   LR L    R  RL R
```

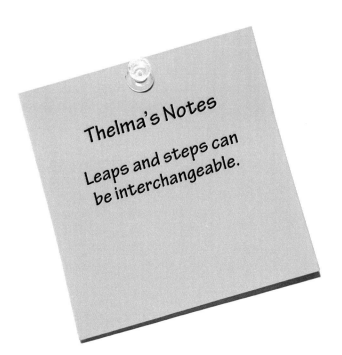

Thelma's Notes

Leaps and steps can be interchangeable.

a1 a2 a3

LEVEL IV - AGES 9–11

Get Ready: This level marks an important transition to a center-floor warm-up. Dancers begin by walking around the room, on either the quarter note or eighth note, and, upon direction from the teacher, moving to a place to dance. Following the Rudiment, Double Heel, Paddle and Roll, and Spank Series, dancers assume the Ready position for the Shuffle Series.

Goal: To increase tempo and clarity and emphasize **FINISHING THE SHUFFLE**! To combine shuffles with other single and double sound movements.

Technique: Be careful to maintain the relaxed ankle, knee and hip, always reinforcing the Release, Relax, Ready concept.

Music Recommendation:
"Tuxedo Junction" (David Leonhardt Trio)

NINE

As in previous levels, begin with simple brushes and spanks in different phrases, sending the leg to different places so that these movements can stand apart from shuffles. Repeat exercises "a.–l." in the brush/spank/shuffle progressions in the previous levels. The difference is that dancers need to change feet more often than when they were at the barre; the simplest solution is to step or hop step. When doing the consecutive shuffles, as in "l.," do them in parallel, crossed in front, to the side and to the back. Add the following to the series:

m. a1 a2...   a7 a   8
    sh BC 7x with sh hop st to change feet   REPEAT on L
    R RL   R L   R
    Break down to:
    sh BC 3x with sh hop st to change feet REPEAT on L [a1 a2 a3 a4 a5 a6 a7 a8]
    sh BC 1x with sh hop st to change feet REPEAT on L [a1 a2 a3 a4]

n. a1 a   2   a3 a4 a5 a6 a7 a8
    sh hop st (in place, forward and back and crossed)
    R L   R
    Note addition to this exercise in Level V.

o. Preparation for adding hop before shuffle; practice at barre before center floor.
    (1)   &a 2 (3)   &a 4
    release sh tdig release sh tdig   REPEAT and REVERSE
    R   R R   R   R R

TEN - *Hop before the shuffle*

Before dancers can do triple time steps, they need to be able to place the hop before the shuffle. This can be challenging for some students, but once mastered, they have a strong base for time-step work. Ensure that dancers are taking off from one foot and playing the rhythm [1&a2] accurately. To prepare dancers for this change, it's helpful to practice this sequence of drills. It may take several weeks before dancers are ready for the last phrase. Make sure they are hopping on one foot and not pushing off from two feet.

p. Hop L shuffle R toe dig R (touch & release) [1&a2 (3 4)] REPEAT
q. Hop L shuffle R toe dig R (release right away) [1&a2 (3) 4&a5 (6) 7&a8] REPEAT
r. Hop L shuffle R step R (shift weight fully and release other foot) [1&a2 (3 4)] REVERSE
s. Hop L shuffle R step R (shift/release) [1&a2 (3) 4&a5 (6) 7&a8]
t. Hop L shuffle R step R (shift/release) [1&a2 3&a4 5&a6 7&a8]

SEE Part ONE, Level IV, for more shuffle
patterns and for classic shuffle steps:
★Waltz Clog
★Buffalo
★Maxie Ford
★Shim Sham
★Irish

Thelma's Notes

Have dancers demonstrate individually to be sure they are finishing their shuffles and articulating hops!

LEVEL V - AGES 10–12

Get Ready: Class again begins with walking and small footwork, then moves to brushes, spanks and shuffles.

Goal: To increase tempo, clarity of rhythm and quality of sound; to strengthen hop before and after the shuffle; to add running triplets to shuffle exercise and choreography.

Technique: Increase challenges slowly, emphasizing relaxed ankles, knees and hips over speed. **If good technique gets lost, students will be stuck at this level and won't progress.**

Music Recommendation:
"Isn't She Lovely" (Stevie Wonder) This is a slow/moderate swing and will allow dancers to focus on technique. It's also long and will allow the teacher to cover all of the shuffle exercises.

ELEVEN - *Double shuffles*

Repeat all Level IV shuffle exercises at center floor. After "l." (swinging shuffles [a1a2a3]), add the following extension to drill "m." Do shuffles in parallel, crossed, to the side and to the back. This exercise can take a full 64 bars if you repeat it in all directions.

```
m. 1&a2  3&a4  5&a6  a7  8
   sh sh  sh sh  sh sh  BC  st  REVERSE
   R  R   R  R   R  R   RL  R
```

```
   1&  a2 a3  4   5&a6  a7  8
   sh sh BC  st     REVERSE
   R  R  RL  R   L   L   LR  L
```

```
   1&a2 a3  4&a5  a6  a7  8
   sh sh BC sh sh BC sh st    REVERSE entire pattern
   R  R  RL R  R  RL R  R
```

Double shuffle with a toe dig:
```
a1 &a 2    (3)        a4  &a  5   (6)        a7 &a 8   REVERSE
sh sh tdig release    sh  sh  tdig release   sh sh  st
R  R  R    R          R   R   R    R         R  R   R
```

Proceed with shuffle hops (drill "n." in Level IV). Be sure to review the hop before the shuffle (drills "p.–t.") so that dancers are getting ready for triple time steps.

TWELVE

+Leap: dancers are learning to play triplets and are ready for **"running" shuffles**.
```
1    &a 2    &a 3    &a 4    &a 5    &a 6    &a 7  a8
leap sh leap sh leap sh leap sh leap sh leap sh  st BC   REVERSE
R    L  L    R  R    L  L    R  R    L  L    R   R  LR
```

THIRTEEN

★Military Time Step:
```
e&a  1  & 2  e&a 3 & 4  e&a  5 e&a  6 e&a  7 & 8
sh hop st st st  [REVERSE] sh hop st sh  hop st sh  hop st st st   REVERSE and REPEAT
R  L   R  R L R  L R L R L  R  L   R  L   R  L  R   L  R  L  R L R
```

The
SLAP &
FLAP
SERIES

The Slap and Flap Series addresses the challenge of combining a brush with a tap (slap) and a brush with a step (flap). These two tap ideas sound the same and are often "played" in the same rhythms. I do not introduce the combination of a brush with a single tap until Level II because I want my Level I dancers to master the individual brush sound they use in the shuffle and the ball tap sound they use in simple choreography. I do not introduce the flap until Level III, as it requires multiple techniques that are developing in Level II (shifting weight, staying on the ball of the foot, releasing to the Ready position).

LEVEL II - AGES 7 & 8

Goal: To combine a brush with a tap in both quarter and eighth-note time. With no weight on the tap, this combination of movements is called a SLAP.
Slap = brush + tap (no weight).

Technique: Do not rush into this until all Level I skills are mastered and Level II ball change and shuffle skills are developing. Have dancers stand in Ready position at the barre, brush out and tap down. Be sure dancers are firmly placing the toe tap to the floor and that knee is not locked, although it is reaching forward or to side as dancers progress. Begin in quarter-note time, being careful that dancers are maintaining a relaxed foot and ankle and, when sounds are clear, progress rhythmically. In the across-the-floor exercise the dancers should fully shift their weight on the heel drop, at the same time Releasing the alternate foot to the Ready position for the next slap.

Music Recommendations:
"Satin Doll" ("Tap Those Feet," Statler) - swing
"Twinkle Twinkle Little Star" - straight

Teaching Slaps:
Say "*con-nect*" in the different rhythms to indicate the connection of the toe tap to the floor. Keep the foot relaxed as it swings out and down. At the barre, front and side: progress from the simplest to the more complex as dancers are demonstrating good technique. Practice on both sides.

1	(2)	3	(456) (7 8)
1	2	(3)	(4)
&	1	(2 3)	(4)
&	1	(2)	(3) - use tune in waltz time
&	1		(2)
a	1		(2) - use swing tune
brush	tap	(wait)	return to *Ready*
R	R		

ONE

ATF: Dancers at this level are usually not fully shifting weight, so although this movement of the slap transitions to a flap, I still say "slap heel." As they start shifting regularly on the step and heel-drop rudiments with a *Relaxed Release*, they are ready to be introduced to the flap.
See Level III Slap and Flap Series

+Heel Drop
Practice these rhythms in place **with no weight,** releasing the slap foot, and also **shifting weight on the heel** and traveling across the floor. Once technique is strengthened, dancers will swing the slap [a1].

No weight change - stay in place:

&1	2	(3 4)
sl	hdrp	RELEASE and REPEAT (practice on L also)
R	R	R

Shift weight on heel drop:

&1	2	(3 4)
sl	hdrp	RELEASE to REVERSE
R	R	L

ATF: These slaps can also swing [a1]. Straight time is noted.

&1	2	(3)	&4	5	(6)	&7	8	(1)	&2	3	(4)	&5	6	7	8	
sl	hdrp		sl	hdrp		sl	hdrp		sl	hdrp		sl	hdrp	st	st	RELEASE to REVERSE
R	R		L	L		R	R		L	L		R	R	L	R	

&5 6 7 8

LEVEL III - AGES 8 & 9

Goal: To transfer weight to the step following a brush to the front or side.
Flap = brush + step (with weight). While focusing here on the introduction of the flap, the slap continues to be developed through exercises included in the Double Heel Series. Dancers will master three consecutive swinging flaps and work primarily in swing time.

Technique: Initially, dancers stay at the barre and strengthen their ability to brush onto the ball of the foot, bringing the opposite foot to the Ready position and then stepping back onto the ball of that foot, repeating this movement on one side and progressing rhythmically. Once dancers are swinging their brush step [a1] with confidence and clarity on both sides and staying on the balls of their feet, they are ready to take their flaps away from the barre. When dancers travel across the floor, emphasize the importance of starting the flap from the Ready position with the foot Relaxed and the knee lifted. At this level, an additional goal is to add a double heel drop (see Double Heel Series).

Music Recommendations:
"Jeepers Creepers" (Maria Maldaur) - swing
"A Bicycle Built for Two" ("Kidsongs") - waltz

Teaching Flaps:
Continue to drill slaps and then shift weight on the steps in the progressive rhythms below. Say
Q"Go there! Step back!" Encourage small movements with foot in a *Relaxed* and *Ready* position
with every step. Watch for locked knees. Practice on both sides.

1	2	(3)	4	
1	&	(2)	3	(4)
1	&		2	(3) - waltz time
1	&		2	(3 4) - straight time
a	1	(2)	3	(4) - swing time
a	1		2	(3 4)
a	1		2	No wait. Move away from barre once this is mastered.
brush	step	(wait)	step back	(wait)
R	R		L	

🩰 TWO

ATF: Begin by alternating a flap with a step so dancers can focus on one side at a time. This pattern is called:

⭐**VARSITY DRAG:**
```
a1 2  a3 4  a5 6  a7 (8)                        a8
fl  st fl  st fl  st fl (wait)  REVERSE; when ready add BC
R  L  R  L  R  L  R                             LR
```

Break down to 4 counts traveling R and L; add arms pushing up and down, alternating R and L.
```
a1 2  a3 a4 a5 6  a7 a8
fl  st fl  BC fl  st fl  BC
R  L  R  LR L  R  L  RL
```

Once dancers are shifting weight on both sides, it's time to practice consecutive flaps. Keep movements small, on the balls of the feet, and make sure dancers are shifting weight and *Releasing* to a *Ready* position before each flap. Vocalize so dancers are reminded of what you expect to see. Adjust the tempo to ensure clear sounds. Add ball change after the third flap when dancers are ready.

♫ "*And lift and lift and lift .… and lift and lift and lift*"								a4 [LR]
a1	a2	a3	(4) a5	a6	a7 (8)			a8 [RL]
fl	fl	fl	fl	fl	fl	(continue ATF; add BC when ready)		
R	L	R	L	R	L			

+Ball Change:
Begin by reviewing step ball change and ensuring that dancers are staying on the balls of their feet and transferring their weight accurately. Make sure dancers are starting their flaps from a *Ready* position, lifting the foot after the ball change. Working at a slow tempo, replace the step with a flap, reinforcing the weight shift and staying on the balls of the feet. Continue to use action words like "*con-nect*," "*go there*" or "*step up*" to inspire your dancers and reinforce the rhythm you want to hear. Make sure your dancers listen to your sounds and that you use "Call and Response" to model the movement and the sound.

♫ "*Pick UP your feet, Pick UP your feet, Pick UP your feet, re-lease*"								
a1	a2	a3	a4	a5	a6	7	8	
fl	BC	fl	BC	fl	BC	st	st	REVERSE
R	LR	L	RL	R	LR	L	R	

+Heel Drop:
Now that dancers are transferring their weight to the ball of the foot on the flap, the flap and heel-drop pattern can be further developed. After reviewing heel-drop exercise TWO in the Level II series, progress to the following rhythms:

ATF:

a1	2	a3	4	a5	6	a7	8	
fl	hdrp	fl	hdrp	fl	hdrp	fl	hdrp	REPEAT
R	R	L	L	R	R	L	L	

a1	a2	a3	4	a5	a6	a7	8	
fl	fl	fl	hdrp	fl	fl	fl	hdrp	REPEAT
R	L	R	R	L	R	L	L	

See Combos (in Part One of this manual) and the Double Heel Series (in Part Two) for more ideas.

a1 2 a3

LEVEL IV - AGES 9–11

Goal: To complete eight or more swinging flaps in place and/or traveling. To be able to play flaps in straight and swing time as part of the Spank Series, the Double Heel Series and the Time Step Series, and to combine with cramp rolls, shuffles, ball changes and single sounds like heel drops, steps and hops.

Technique: Continue to reinforce the *Release, Relax, Ready* principle so that flaps take off from no weight and shift immediately to having weight. The action should go downward, and if the intention is to travel, the body should move with the action foot, shifting the knee, hip and scapula over the flapping foot. If the intention is to stay in place, dancers should lift the knee and brush right under the body. The brush of the flap becomes almost a light tap. When learning "running flaps" some dancers benefit from practicing in front of a wall so that they remain in place.

Music Recommendations:

"That's Entertainment" ("Music for Tap Dancing," Kimbo) - swing

🥿 THREE - "Running" flaps

Continue to review Slap and Flap Series Levels II and III, emphasizing a light brush step and practicing both straight and swinging rhythms. This next exercise strengthens flaps in place, which alternate with traveling flaps every 4 counts. You may want to begin with alternating 8 counts. When dancers are improving, alternate every 2 counts.

```
a1  a2  a3 a4  a5  a6  a7  a8
fl   fl    fl   fl    fl   fl    fl    fl   REPEAT, alternating staying in place with traveling
R   L   R   L   R   L   R   L
[in  place  ] [traveling forward]
```

🥿 FOUR

This exercise is similar to the pattern of a Varsity Drag but can be done straight or syncopated. Initially drill this as an across-the-floor exercise; later it can become part of a combo.

```
a1  a   2a  3   a4  a   5a  6   a7  a (8)              a8 - swing
&1  &   2&  3   &4  &   5&  6   &7  8                  &8 - straight
fl   st   fl   st   fl   st   fl   st   fl   st   REPEAT or do BC to REVERSE
R   L   R   L   R   L   R   L   R   L                  LR
```

See Time Step Series, Spank Series and Double Heel Series for additional flap work.

LEVEL V - AGES 10–12

Goal: By this time, dancers are using flaps with time steps and cramp rolls and in place of steps in many combinations, particularly those that travel. At this level, dancers are working on fine-tuning the flap so that it swings easily from the *Ready* position and can move or stay in place. One goal is to flap to the side from a crossed-front position, as in the Buffalo. Another goal is to move backward while flapping, using what we can call "running" flaps (which leap to the step after the brush). Dancers also work toward running eighth-note triplets.

Technique: The *Release* to a *Ready* position remains a critical factor in teaching good flaps. As the flaps in time steps and other combinations need to remain under the dancer, lifting the knee and brushing lightly will result in a relaxed double sound.

Music Recommendations:
"A Kiss to Build a Dream On" (Trio de Swing)

FIVE

Continue to drill all of the previous flap exercises, particularly exercises THREE and FOUR in Level IV. Add the following variation to exercise THREE. Begin in the front of the room so there is space to travel backwards. Be sure to brush forward despite traveling back.

```
a1 a2 a3 a4  a5 a6 a7 a8
fl  fl  fl  fl   fl  fl  fl   fl   REPEAT  Alternate 4 cts. in place with 4 cts. traveling backwards.
R  L R  L   R  L R  L
[in  place ]   [travel back]
```

SIX

This exercise introduces flaps in running eighth-note triplets. Again, the more Relaxed and Ready the dancer is, the easier this exercise will be.

ATF:
```
a1&a2   a3&a4    a5&a6  a7&a8
fl  fl st   fl  fl st    REPEAT
R L R   L R L
```

Add the longer continuation once the above is mastered:
```
a1&a 2    a3&a4   a5&  a6&  a7&  a8
fl  fl   st  fl  fl   st fl st  fl st   fl st  fl   REVERSE
R L   R L R  L R L R L   R L  R
```

This next continuation/phrase can also be added to the first idea:
```
a1 &a 2   a3 &a 4   a5 &a 6&  a7 &a 8
fl  fl   st  fl  fl   st  fl  fl   fl  fl   fl st   REPEAT
R L   R L R   L R L R  L R L
```

The
PADDLE &
ROLL
SERIES

LEVEL IV - AGES 9–11

I do not recommend teaching the 4-sound combination of the heel dig, spank, toe dig, heel drop, also known as a paradiddle, in the three early levels. Young tappers are unlikely to have the facility to perform this movement **with good technique,** except in quarter-note time, and there are many other tap movements that they can develop and strengthen. Years of careful attention to technique will enable them to learn paddle and rolls quickly and successfully in Level IV.

Before introducing the paddle and roll, be sure that your dancers are able to:

• *Release* the alternate foot to a *Relaxed* and *Ready* position following a heel drop.

• Perform step heel-drop rudiments in eighth-note time (See Rudiment Series).

• Perform the Level IV Spank Series (See Spank Series).

• Present a heel dig without locking the knee.

Teaching the Paddle and Roll (PDRL, when starting with a heel dig)

Teach a cappella or accompany with a drum so you can adjust tempo easily.

STEP ONE: For beginners, start with the heel dig and spank exercise below. This first exercise should be done in quarter-note time until dancers are ready to progress. Once they are demonstrating good technique, with the *Release* of a *Relaxed* ankle on the spank, they can combine quarter and eighth notes as indicated.

```
1    2  3   4 5  & 6  & 7   & 8  &
hdig sp hdig sp hdig sp hdig sp hdig sp hdig sp  REPEAT   (step on ct. 8 to REVERSE)
R    R  R   R R  R R  R R  R R  R
```

STEP TWO: Isolate each sound and make sure the ankle, knee and hip are *Relaxed* and the spank from the heel dig to the toe dig goes up and then presses down onto the ball tap. Practice in quarter-note time before progressing to eighth notes. Lift to the *Ready* position on the silent notes.

```
1    2  3   (4) 5   6  7  (8)
hdig sp tdig    hdig sp tdig   4x  (drop heel on ct. 8 to RELEASE/REVERSE)
R    R  R       R  R  R
```

STEP THREE: Progress to eighth notes, emphasizing a strong toe dig.
RELEASE and REVERSE on final heel drop to change feet.

```
1  & 2  (3) 4  & 5  (6) 7  & 8  (1) 2  & 3  (4) 5  & 6  (7) 8
hdig sp tdig  hdig sp tdig   hdig sp tdig   hdig sp tdig   hdig sp tdig   hdrp REVERSE
R  R  R     R  R  R      R  R  R      R  R  R      R  R  R      R
```

STEP FOUR: Add the heel drop, making sure the toe dig is strong and followed by a *Release* to a *Relaxed* foot in the *Ready* position at the same time as the heel drop. Work in quarter-note time before progressing to STEP FIVE.

```
1    2  3    4
hdig sp tdig hdrp  (wait if necessary to assure readiness, then REVERSE)
R    R  R    R
```

STEP FIVE: Increase the tempo slowly through the following rhythm progressions. Do not proceed to the next rhythm until dancers have mastered the preceding one.

```
1       2     &     3      (4) REVERSE [5 6 & 7 (8)]
1       &     2     3      (4) REVERSE [5 & 6 7 (8)]
1       & (2) 3     &      (4) REVERSE [5 & (6) 7 & (8)]
1       &     2     &      (3) REVERSE [4 & 5 & (6) REVERSE 7 & 8 &]
hdig    sp    tdig  hdrp   RELEASE
R       R     R     R
```

ONE

The following pattern incorporates a clap and a step and is an example of an exercise that keeps the paddle and roll articulate.

Have dancers say, "*Paddle and a step clap, paddle and a step clap, paddle and a paddle and a paddle and a dig clap.*"

```
1&2&  3 4    5&6&  7  8    1&2&  3&4&  5&6&  7    8
PDRL st clap PDRL  st  clap PDRL PDRL PDRL tdig clap  RELEASE L to REVERSE
RRRR L        RRRR L         RRRR LLLL  RRRR L
```

CHALLENGE:
Substitute a paddle and roll for the shuffle step heel drop in exercise THIRTEEN of the Rudiment Series.

LEVEL V - AGES 10–12

Goal: To play the four-sound paddle and roll combination in eighth-note time beginning with either the heel dig (hdig) or the heel drop (hdrp).

Technique: Reinforce the technique of *Releasing* a *Relaxed* foot by working at slow tempos and reviewing the exercises in Level IV. Ensure that dancers are articulating each sound and playing the notes accurately. Continue to drill basic rudiment and spank exercises to strengthen the components of the paddle and roll.

Music Recommendations:
"Cantaloop" ("Hand on the Torch," Us 3)
"Watermelon Man" (Pancho Sanchez and Mongo Santamaria)
"The Girl from Ipanema" (David Leonhardt Trio) or other Latin-style tunes

Before progressing, review exercises in Level IV Paddle and Roll Series. Isolate each sound and make sure the ankle, knee and hip are relaxed and the spank from the heel dig to the toe dig goes up and then presses down onto the ball tap. Practice first in quarter-note time before progressing to eighth notes. As in other series, progress systematically by first combining quarter and eighth notes before moving to all eighth notes.

TWO – *Begin in quarter note time and double up when dancers are ready.*

```
1    2    3    4      5    &    6    &    7    &    8    &
hdig sp   tdig hdrp   hdig sp   tdig hdrp hdig sp   tdig hdrp  REVERSE
R    R    R    R      L    L    L    L    R    R    R    R
```

THREE – *Put three paddles together with steps.*

```
1&2&   3&4&   5&6&   7  8
PDRL   PDRL   PDRL   st st  REVERSE
RRRR   LLLL   RRRR   L  R
```

FOUR – *Introduce the paddle that starts with a heel drop.*

Dancers must be *Releasing* to a *Relaxed* foot and able to shift weight clearly on heel drops. Practice first in quarter-note time and then progress to a combination and then to all eighth notes.

```
1    2    3    4    5    6    7    8
hdrp hdig sp   tdig hdrp hdig sp   tdig
L    R    R    R    L    L
```

```
1    2    3    4    5    &    6    &    7    &    8    &
hdrp hdig sp   tdig hdrp hdig sp   tdig hdrp hdig sp   tdig
L    R    R    R    L    L    L    L    R    R
```

REVERSE all above

```
1    &    2    &    3    &    4    &    5    &    6    &    7    &    8    &
hdrp hdig sp   tdig hdrp hdig sp   tdig hdrp hdig sp   tdig hdrp hdig sp   tdig  REPEAT
L    R    R    R    L    L    L    L    R    R    R    R    L    L
```

REVERSE by stopping on count 7 and repeating that heel drop on count 1.

1 2 3 4 5

The
SPANK
SERIES

LEVEL IV - AGES 9–11

Prior to this level, spanks are usually done following a brush, as in a shuffle.

Goal:.To introduce the spank that begins on the floor. The back brush (spank) has usually started with the toe tap released, following a brush or heel dig. By now, dancers can isolate the toe and understand the concept of *Release* (rudiment exercises). In preparation for learning paddle and rolls, drawbacks and pullbacks, dancers must be able to brush up from the floor without first lifting the foot.

Technique: The *Relaxed* ankle/foot continues to play an important part in the success of this new skill. The Spank Series was adapted from one of Brenda Bufalino's footwork exercises. Be watchful for the dancer who moves the heel dig forward in order to *Release* the toe. The heel stays firmly planted into the floor and the toe tap simply *Releases*. It's helpful for dancers to place the action foot in front of the standing leg while learning this skill.

Music Recommendations:
"Sham Time" (Ronnie Laws) - straight
"I've Got the World on a String" (Beegie Adair) - swing
"Tap, Tap" ("Tap Dance Kid," Broadway original cast) - soft shoe

Teaching Spanks from the Floor:

STEP ONE: with R foot placed slightly in front of L, weight evenly distributed, ankle relaxed.

1	2	3	4
RELEASE ball tap,	sp (lifting up,not back),	tdig (place in front),	hdrp
R	R	R	R

Repeat until technique of releasing toe/ball and placing dig is understood. Change feet by bringing the last toe dig back and releasing opposite toe at the same time as the heel drops. Progress rhythmically. Practice new rhythms with repetitions on the same foot before changing feet.

STEP TWO:
Dancers will progress quickly from quarter notes to eighth notes, but don't skip rhythm "**a.**"! Proper technique is necessary for long-term progress.

Practice "**a.**" until the technique of *Release* and placement is mastered. Progress to "**b.**" when dancers are ready. Upon mastery of "**b.**," proceed to running eighth notes "**c.**".

a.	1	2	3	4	5	6	7	8
b.	&	1	&	2	&	3	&	4... bring to back on 7 & 8 to REVERSE.
c.		1	&	2		&	3	&... bring to back on 7 & 8 to REVERSE.
	RELEASE	sp	tdig	hdrp	RELEASE	sp	tdig	hdrp
	R	R	R	R	R		R	R R

Once mastered, change feet by stepping back on LAST toe dig, heel drop (AST releasing opposite toe as weight shifts to the heel drop).

ONE - *Change feet and alternate with brush step forward.*

```
1    & 2    3 & 4    5 & 6    7 & 8
sp   st hdrp sp  st hdrp sp  st hdrp sp  st hdrp
R    R R    L  L L    R  R R    L  L L
```

REPEAT rhythm traveling forward on the right, replacing the spank with a brush step heel drop. Continue the pattern of traveling back and forward. (To travel back, *Release* the toe of the foot that played count 8).

```
1    & 2    & 3 &  4    & 5  &  6 &   7 & 8
sp   st hdrp sp  st hdrp sp   st hdrp sp  st hdrp sp  st hdrp
R    R R    L L  L    R   R R    L L  L    R  R R
```

```
1 & 2   & 3 &   4 & 5   & 6 &    7 & 8
br st hdrp br  st hdrp br  st  hdrp br  st hdrp br  st hdrp
L  L L    R  R R    L L  L    R  R R    L L  L
```

REVERSE and REPEAT

TWO - *Alternate rhythms.*

Traveling forward or back, changing feet with each spank or brush:

```
1 &  2    3&45&67&8 alternate with 1   & 2     &3&4&5&6&7&8
sp st hdrp 4x                      sp st hdrp 5x traveling backward
br st  hdrp 4x                     br st hdrp 5x traveling forward
```

THREE - *Alternate placements.*

```
1   & 2    & 3 &   4
sp  st hdrp sp  st hdrp sp
R   R R    L  L L    R
```

```
5 &   6  & 7    & 8
st hdrp sp  st hdrp sp  st
R  R    L  L L    R  R
```

```
1    & 2 &  3  & 4    & 5 &   6 & 7   (8)
hdrp sp  st hdrp sp  st  hdrp sp  st hdrp sp  st hdrp clap
R    L  L L    R  R R    L  L L    R  R R    RELEASE L
```

REPEAT the rhythms traveling forward with left brush in place of the spank.

RELEASE the toe of the last heel drop on count 7 after traveling forward. REVERSE to spanks traveling back, starting with L.

SPANK SERIES - LEVEL IV

LEVEL V - AGES 10-12

Goal: To draw the spank up from the floor without kicking out the whole foot. To continue to strengthen all brush and spank patterns, introducing drawback and paddle ideas and bringing brushes and spanks into classic choreography such as soft shoe and time steps. To increase tempo of basic exercises and use swing tunes, playing the eighth-note triplets.

Technique: Continue to emphasize *Relaxation*, *Release* and *Readiness* to spank (brush up) from the floor with ease. As dancers are maturing, it is important that they keep their weight over the arch so that either the heel or the toe can be released.

Music Recommendations:
"Sidewinder" (Eddie Harris) - straight
"Funky Big Band" (Janet Jackson) - swing
"Friends to the End" ("Toy Story" soundtrack) - soft shoe

FOUR - *Repetitions on same foot: place toe dig slightly in front.*

```
&  a  1    (2)       &  a  3    (4)       & a 5 (6) & a 7 (8)
sp tdig hdrp RELEASE sp tdig hdrp  RELEASE   REPEAT
R  R   R             R  R   R
```

```
&  a  1  &  a  2  &  a  3  &  a  4    & a 5 & a 6 & a 7 & a 8
sp tdig hdrp sp tdig hdrp sp tdig hdrp sp tdig hdrp  REPEAT
R  R   R  R  R   R  R  R   R  R  R   R
```

REVERSE to the other foot by placing the last spank step and heel drop back and releasing the opposite toe.

FIVE - *Change feet.*

REPEAT above exercise traveling back, changing feet with each spank playing the above rhythms alternately, as in exercise TWO. Repeat the exercise traveling forward with brushes, starting on right. RELEASE the toe of the last heel drop after traveling forward with brushes to REVERSE to spanks traveling back, starting with L.

SIX

This is a continuation with alternate placement of the spank/brush, the step and the heel drop, as in exercise THREE, traveling back (spank) and forward (brush):

```
1 & a    2 & a   3 & a   4
sp st hdrp sp st hdrp sp st hdrp sp
R R R    L L L   R R R   L
```

```
5 &   a 6 &   a 7 &   a 8
st hdrp sp st hdrp sp st hdrp sp st
L L    R R R L L L    R R
```

```
1   & a 2   & a 3   & a 4    & a 5   & a 6   & a 7   & a 8
hdrp sp st hdrp sp st hdrp sp st hdrp sp st hdrp sp st hdrp sp st hdrp sp st hdrp
R    L L L    R R R    L L L    R R R    L L L    R R R    L L L
```

Travel forward (start with R), substituting a brush for a spank.

RELEASE the toe of the last heel drop after traveling forward with brushes to REVERSE to spanks traveling back, starting with L.

1 & a 2 a

SEVEN - Drawbacks (3 sounds).

⭐ **DRAWBACKS** (step spank heel drop) can be introduced once dancers have mastered the skill of drawing the spank up from a flat foot. Level V is a good time to introduce this concept because Level IV students often confuse the spank exercise (all on one foot) with the drawback, which incorporates the same three ideas, but in a different order. As with other skills, begin in quarter-note time, increasing tempo and rhythmic challenge by working with both straight and swing tunes. Drawbacks (three sounds) are a great example of a movement that correlates with eighth-note triplets (three beats).

Progressive Rhythmic Exercises to Teach DRAWBACKS:

STEP ONE: Practice stepping back and AST releasing the toe, in 3 count phrases.
```
1  2   3   (4) 5  6   7      (8)
st sp  hdrp    st sp  hdrp
R  L   R       L  R   L
```

STEP TWO: Start with step on count 1, traveling back. Practice on both sides.
```
1 2 3    4 5 6   7 8
st sp hdrp st sp hdrp st st
R  L R    L R  L  R  L
```

STEP THREE: Introduce eighth notes.
```
1 & 2    3 & 4    5 & 6    7 & 8
st sp hdrp st sp hdrp st sp hdrp st sp hdrp
R  L  R    L  R  L    R  L  R    L  R  L
```

STEP FOUR: Play straight eighth notes. Practice on both sides.
```
1 & 2   & 3 &   4 & 5   & 6 &   7  8
st sp hdrp st sp hdrp st sp hdrp st sp hdrp st  STA REPEAT
R  L  R    L  R  L    R  L  R    L  R  L    R  L
```

STEP FIVE: Introduce eighth-note triplets by first playing step heel drops in swing time.
```
1  a   2  a   3  a   4  a   5  a   6  a   7  a   8  a
st hdrp st hdrp st hdrp st hdrp st hdrp st hdrp st hdrp st  hdrp  REPEAT
R  R   L  L    R  R   L  L    R  R   L  L    R  R   L  L
```

STEP SIX: Insert the spank between the step and the heel drop.
```
1 & a    2 & a    3 & a    4 & a    5 & a   6 & a    7 & a    8 & a
st sp hdrp st sp hdrp st sp hdrp st sp hdrp st sp hdrp st sp hdrp st sp hdrp st sp hdrp  REPEAT
R  L  R    L  R  L    R  L  R    L  R  L    R  L  R    L  R  L    R  L  R    L  R  L
```

⭐ **CINCINNATI:** Once drawbacks are mastered, dancers can be challenged with other classic tap choreography. The shuffle opens to the side.

a	1		&a	2	a	3		&a	4	a5	&	a6	a7	&	a8
sp	hdrp	sh	st		sp	hdrp	sh	st	REPEAT						
R	L		R		R	L		R		L		L			

⭐ **DOUBLE CINCINNATI:**
ATF: traveling backwards.

1	&	a	2&	a	3	&	a	4&	a	5	&	a	6&	a	7	&	a	8
st	sp	hdrp	sh	hdrp	st	sp	hdrp	sh	hdrp	st	sp	hdrp	sh	hdrp	st	sp	hdrp	st	REVERSE
R	L	R		L	R		L	R	L		R	L		R	L	R		L	R		L	R	L		R

⭐ **SOFT-SHOE STEPS:** See Combos and The Next Step in Part One, Levels IV and V.
The following soft-shoe steps are an integral part of Levels IV and V. As the spank is mastered, insert it and/or a brush whenever possible. Flaps are also added in place of steps.

Single Essence: step brush ball change, crossing front
Double Essence: step brush ball change, spank ball change, brush ball change
Back Essence: spank step ball change (open to 2nd position on ball change)
Paddle turn: flap brush ball change, brush ball change, brush ball change (inside turn)
Paddle turn: flap spank ball change, spank ball change, spank ball change (outside turn)
Grapevine step: see one example below.

⭐ **GRAPEVINE:** Movement alternates crossing front and back.

a	1	a	2	a	3	a4	a	5	a6	a7	a	8	
sp	hdrp	br	hdrp	sp	hdrp	fl	sp	st	BC	BC	st	STO	REVERSE
RXBL	L	Rside	L	RXFL	L	R	LXBR	L	RXBL	RXFL	R	L	

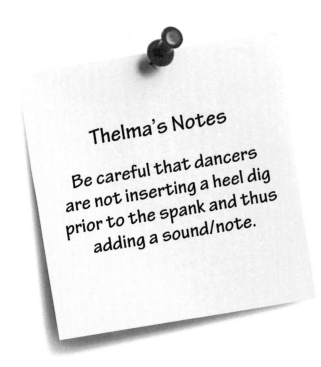

Thelma's Notes

Be careful that dancers are not inserting a heel dig prior to the spank and thus adding a sound/note.

The
TIME
STEP
SERIES

Time Steps: As their shuffles and stomps strengthen, dancers can be introduced to the traditional time step, which, depending on your intention, can start with a shuffle or a stomp. Time steps that start with a stomp are sometimes called "Buck Time Steps." Dancers should be trained to do both the stomp and the shuffle. At this level I focus on just the single time step to ensure good technique.

LEVEL IV - AGES 9–11

Goal: To learn the traditional single time step.

Technique: Except for the stomp, all traditional time-step work is done on the balls of the feet. Dancers keep their hips, knees and ankles relaxed so as to "sit into" the floor, protecting their bodies from injury.

Music Recommendations:
"I'm Beginning to See the Light" (Anne Hampton Callaway)

Teaching Time Steps:

The following short phrases can establish the weight shifts important to the success of learning time steps. These progressive drills/exercises can be done in place or traveling forward and back and should be practiced on both sides. To be sure dancers are Releasing and not shifting weight to the stomp, I recommend starting with a shuffle. Eventually the stomp and spank can replace the shuffle. These phrases become the single time step at this level. In Level V, the second flap and the shuffle replace the single step after the hop to become double and triple time steps. When teaching time steps at this level, I keep the rhythms straight to ensure clarity. Practice these preliminary drills on both sides.

```
8& l    2 (3)  4&5 6 (7)
sh hop st      REVERSE
R  L   R
```

```
8&1    2  3    4&5 6 7
sh hop st st   REPEAT (keep the steps in place)
R  L   R  L
```

```
(8 1)   2 &3  &  (4 5) 6&7&
        st fl  st       REVERSE
        R  L   R
```

I sometimes use this next drill as a **simple single time step** and **accent** the step.

```
(8) 1    2  &3 & (4) 5 6&7&
    hop st fl st    REVERSE
    L   R  L  R
```

```
8    1    2 (3) 4 5 6 (7)
STO hop st      REVERSE
R    L   R
```

```
8    1 (2) 3 & 4    5 (6) 7 &
STO hop st st STO hop   st st REPEAT
R    L    R L R  L      R L
```

Thelma's Notes

Remind dancers to stay on the balls of the feet except when stomping.

ONE

⭐ **SINGLE TIME STEP:** This is the simple version before a spank and a flap are added.

```
8     1   2   3   &   4 5 6 7&
STO  hop st  st  st  REVERSE
R    L   R   L   R
```

```
8&1   2   3   &   4&5 6 7&
sh hop st  st  st  REVERSE
R L   R   L   R
```

Once the spank is mastered and the flap is strengthened, the time step becomes:

```
8     &   1    2 &3 &
STO  sp  hop st fl  st  REVERSE (The stomp and spank can be replaced with a shuffle [8&].)
R    R   L   R L  R
```

HALF BREAK (after completing 7 single time steps):

```
4     &   5   &6  &7 (8)
STO  sp  hop fl   BC
L    L   R   L    RL
```

LEVEL V - AGES 10–12

Goal: The traditional single time step is introduced in Level IV in straight time. In Level V, as the spank is being strengthened, teachers can alternate between straight and swinging time steps, with the "swing" happening on the spank of the shuffle or the spank following the stomp, on the brush of the flap and on the step following the flap. Musical notations below are for swinging the double and triple time steps and breaks. Both half breaks and full breaks are provided.

Technique: Dancers can continue to drill the practice exercises in Time Step Series Level IV. Single time steps and breaks should always be reviewed.

Music Recommendations:
"42nd Street" (Broadway original cast)
"Anything Goes" (Broadway original cast)

🩰 TWO

⭐ **DOUBLE TIME STEP:** The stomp and spank can be replaced with a shuffle.

8		a	1		a2	a3	a		4a5	a6	a7	a
STO		sp	hop		fl	fl	st		REVERSE			
R			R		L	R	L		R			

🩰 THREE

⭐ **TRIPLE TIME STEP:** Shuffle opens to the side.

8		a	1	&a	2	a3	a	
STO		sp	hop	sh	st	fl	st	REVERSE
R			R	L	R	R	L	R

🩰 FOUR

Once dancers master the single, double and triple time steps, it is time to introduce breaks (either 4- or 8-count phrases that bring a "punch" to the end of the time step). There is no end to the possible breaks. These are just a few possibilities.

⭐ **HALF BREAKS:** These would replace the 8th time step and would be only 4 counts.

4a	5	a6	a7		4a	5		6	a7	a
sh	st	sh	BC	OR	sh	hop		st	sh	st
L	L	R	RL		L	R		L	R	R

⭐ **FULL BREAKS:** These would follow the 6th time step and would be 8 counts.

8a	1		2	a3	a	4a	5		a6	a7	
sh	hop	st	sh	st		sh	st	sh	BC		
R	L		R	L	L	R	R	R	L	LR	

⭐ **BUCK TIME STEP BREAK:**

8		a	1	2		a3	a	4a	5		a6	a7
STO		sp	hop	st		sh	st	sh	hop	fl		BC
R		R	L	R		L	L	R	L		R	LR

TAP DANCER BIOS

Chloe Arnold is an internationally recognized teacher, choreographer, performer, director, actress and producer based in Los Angeles and New York City. She is known for founding the DC Tap Festival and co-directing the L.A. Tap Festival, as well as founding and choreographing her all-female tap troupe, Syncopated Ladies. Chloe has appeared on such television shows as *So You Think You Can Dance* and *Dancing With the Stars*; in music videos with Beyonce; and in *Imagine Tap!* and Jason Samuels Smith's *Charlie's Angels: A Tribute to Charlie Parker*. A graduate of Columbia University, Chloe runs Chloe & Maud Productions alongside her sister and has her own tap clothing line.

Julia Boynton is a Boston-based teacher, performer and producer who performed with Brian Jones' All-Tap Revue and Heather Cornell's Manhattan Tap. She is co-director of Boston Percussive Dance and founder and director of the annual Beantown Tapfest, Boston's summer tap festival.

Buster Brown (1914–2002) was a teacher, choreographer and performer known for his fast feet and sense of humor. He was a member of the Copasetics – including Charles "Cholly" Atkins, Ernest "Brownie" Brown, Honi Coles, Charles "Cookie" Cook and Pete Nugent – as well as the Hoofers – who included Dr. Jimmy Slyde, Chuck Green and Baby Laurence – and he toured for many years with the orchestras of Duke Ellington, Count Basie, Cab Calloway, Dizzy Gillespie and others. Buster appeared in the Broadway musical *Black and Blue*, the PBS Special *Great Performances: Gregory Hines' Tap Dance in America*, the film *Cotton Club*, and the tap documentary *Great Feats of Feet*. Beginning in 1997, he was the master of ceremonies for a weekly tap jam at Swing 46, a Manhattan jazz club, which he always opened by singing "Gotta Go Tap Dancin'." Buster's signature tune was "Cute," and his routine "Laura" is a classic piece of tap repertoire.

Brenda Bufalino is one of tap's living legends – a multi-talented master teacher, choreographer, soloist and writer. She was the cofounder, choreographer and artistic director of the American Tap Dance Orchestra, which included dancers Barbara Duffy, Margaret Morrison and Tony Waag, and whose choreography, known for its intricate counterpoints, pioneered tap dance in concert form. Brenda collaborated and performed for many years with her mentor, Charles "Honi" Coles, an actor and tap dancer known for his work with Charles "Cholly" Atkins as the duet Coles & Atkins. A resident of New York City, she is Artistic Mentor for the American Tap Dance Foundation and continues to perform and teach workshops around the world.

Leon Collins (1922–1985) was born in Chicago. He began tap dancing at an early age and later worked professionally with groups and big bands (Jimmie Lunceford). In the 1960s, when the popularity of tap waned, he restored cars. In the 1970s Leon came out of retirement and began to teach, opening a studio in Roxbury, MA, with Boston's "First Lady of Jazz," Mae Arnette in 1976. In 1982 Leon and three of his students, Clara Brosnaham ("CB") Hetherington, Dianne Walker and Pamela Raff, opened the Leon Collins Dance Studio Inc., in Brookline, MA. His company, Leon Collins & Co., which included his students and pianist Joan Hill, performed from 1982 until his untimely death, of lung cancer, in 1985. Leon had bit parts in a few movies and worked with jazz, bebop and eventually classical music (in particular, a famous rendition of "Flight of the Bumblebee"). *Songs Unwritten*, a documentary about him produced by David Wadsworth, was released shortly after his death.

Steve Condos (1918–1990) received his initial dance training on the streets of Philadelphia. When his family moved to New York City, he began touring the vaudeville circuit along with brothers Frank and Nick, known collectively as The Condos Brothers. Skilled performers and improvisers, the trio gained national and international fame dancing in Hollywood movie musicals and with the bands of great leaders like Count Basie and Duke Ellington. Steve Condos also appeared in the 1989 movie *Tap*. Later in life, he became a popular teacher at workshops and festivals. His Rudiments, exercises for refining technique and inspiring improvisation, are now a staple of tap classes around the world.

Heather Cornell is best known as the director and choreographer of Manhattan Tap, a concert tap company, predominately active in the 1990s, that launched the careers of many of today's most respected tappers, including Roxanne Butterfly, Josh Hilberman, Jeannie Hill, Michael Minery and Max Pollak. Mentored by tap legends Buster Brown, Eddie Brown, Charles "Cookie" Cook, Steve Condos and Chuck Green, Heather has choreographed most of her work to original music, notably that of bass player Ray Brown. She currently lives and works in upstate New York.

Lynn Dally, artistic director of the Jazz Tap Ensemble, is a recognized leader in the renaissance of tap dance in the U.S. and abroad. Since cofounding the ensemble in 1979, she has created more than 30 original tap choreographies. Based in Los Angeles, Lynn is an adjunct professor in the Department of World Art and Cultures at UCLA.

Dean Diggins is the protégé of Paul Draper, a New York-based dancer known for his uniquely original fusion of ballet and tap. In 1957, Dean formed the Mattison Trio, a balletic tap group that enjoyed a decade of performances on television and on stages nationwide. Now a resident of Kittery, ME, Dean has recently collaborated with Drika Overton on several projects, including the original show *Clara's Dream: A Jazz Nutcracker*.

Michelle Dorrance is a performer, teacher and choreographer based in New York City. The recipient of a 2011 Bessie Award and a 2012 Princess Grace Award, she trained with the North Carolina Youth Tap Ensemble under the mentorship of Gene Medler. Michelle has danced in Savion Glover's Ti Dii, Heather Cornell's Manhattan Tap, *STOMP*, *Imagine Tap!*, Barbara Duffy & Company and Jazz Tap Ensemble. Widely recognized for her quirky style and innovative choreography, Michelle is the founder and artistic director of Dorrance Dance, a NYC-based company, and is considered one of today's top young tap artists.

Barbara Duffy, based in New York City, is known internationally as a dynamic teacher, choreographer and performer. Born and raised in Massachusetts, she studied with the great Leon Collins, whose famous repertoire she continues to share at workshops and master classes, and worked extensively with the late Gregory Hines. From 1986 to 1999, Barbara was dance captain and featured ensemble performer with Brenda Bufalino's American Tap Dance Orchestra, and she currently directs an all-female ensemble, Barbara Duffy & Company. She teaches regularly in NYC, including a class focused solely on improvisation exercises, one of her trademarks.

Sean Fielder, a Boston-based teacher, performer and choreographer was a member of the national tour of *Bring In 'Da Noise, Bring In 'Da Funk*. He is now the founder and artistic director of the Boston Tap Company, a multigenerational troupe that performs in original productions and at local events.

Savion Glover inspired a generation of tap dancers and became the poster child for the art form with his funky, hard-hitting appearances in the 1990s, including a Tony Award-winning role in *Bring In 'Da Noise, Bring In 'Da Funk* and multiple appearances on *Sesame Street*. Taught by such masters as Sammy Davis, Jr., Gregory Hines, Henry LeTang and Jimmy Slyde, Savion made his Broadway debut in *The Tap Dance Kid* at ten years old. He has since performed in many films and television shows, even dubbing the taps for the animated movie *Happy Feet* and its sequel. Savion directs his company, Ti Dii, and often performs alongside his protégé, Marshall Davis, Jr.

Jane Goldberg is a "rara avis": a dancer who is also a writer. She has been one of the most prolific voices in the field of tap dancing for the past three decades. As artistic director of Changing Times Tap, a non-profit preservation, promotion, and performing entity, begun in 1979, Jane began teaching at New York University and giving workshops and master classes to college and serious dance students. Her company produced the first international festival, By Word of Foot, in 1980, at the renowned NYC Village Gate. Her acclaimed memoir, *Shoot Me While I'm Happy: Memories from the Tap Goddess of The Lower East Side*, with an introduction by Gregory Hines, comes with a bonus DVD that highlights this celebration of teaching. Known as "the hoofer with angst," Jane has performed her comedy/tap act, *Rhythm & Schmooze*, "topical tap with running commentary over the feet," in countless jazz, contemporary and experimental venues throughout the United States, such as the Village Vanguard in NYC, the Goodman Theatre in Chicago and Harvard University in Cambridge. She is the recipient of two Fulbright Scholarships to India, where she performed her highly idiosyncratic program throughout the subcontinent.

Derick Grant was an original cast member and dance captain for *Bring In 'Da Noise, Bring In 'Da Funk* and co-creator and choreographer of *Imagine Tap!* An award-winning performer, teacher and choreographer based in New York City, lauded for his creativity and artistry, he was the first tap choreographer invited to work on *So You Think You Can Dance*. Derick is currently a spokesman for SoDanca tap shoes.

Josh Hilberman is an internationally recognized teacher, performer and choreographer, known for infusing his classes and performances with his zany humor. Based until recently in Boston, Josh danced with Heather Cornell's Manhattan Tap and originated the role of the Jazz Nut in Drika Overton's *Clara's Dream: A Jazz Nutcracker*. A mentor for many of today's young tap artists and a popular teacher at festivals, his routine "Cappella Josh" has become a standard piece of tap repertoire around the world.

Jeannie Hill was a founding member of and principal performer with Billy Siegenfeld's Jump Rhythm Jazz Project and toured for seven years with Heather Cornell's Manhattan Tap. Jeannie trained extensively with Bob Audy and originated the role of Clara in the world premiere of Drika Overton's *Clara's Dream*. An accomplished soloist and choreographer, she has been teaching at the University of Wisconsin at Stevens Point since 2004.

Gregory Hines (1946–2003) was a multitalented dancer, actor, singer and choreographer. Born in New York City, he and his older brother Maurice trained under master teacher Henry LeTang and performed together as the Hines Brothers, or, with their father, Maurice Sr., as Hines, Hines and Dad. A skilled improviser with comedic charm, Gregory appeared in films such as *Tap* and *White Nights*; several Broadway musicals, including *Jelly's Last Jam* and *Sophisticated Ladies*; and a PBS "Great Performances" special, *Gregory Hines' Tap Dance in America*, featuring fellow hoofers Tommy Tune, Buster Brown, Jimmy Slyde and Honi Coles. Many of today's tappers, including Jane Goldberg, Barbara Duffy, Savion Glover and Ted Levy, consider Gregory Hines a significant mentor.

Jimmy "Sir Slyde" Mitchell (1928–2008) was an icon of the Boston tap scene who studied under Stanley Brown. As one of the Slyde Brothers, he performed throughout New England alongside Jimmy Slyde, incorporating a gliding style within traditional tap technique.

Drika Overton, a veteran of over 30 years as a tap and percussive dance artist, has been a leader in the resurgence of the vital American art of tap dance. She has been the creative force in the formation of several innovative ensembles, and has produced numerous festivals and events, including *MaD Theatricals*, *Clara's Dream: A Jazz Nutcracker*, and the *Portsmouth Vaudeville Project*, in addition to the Portsmouth Percussive Dance Festival, an internationally recognized week-long summer festival of music, dance and song. Drika currently teaches workshops and produces events at the Dance Hall in Kittery, ME.

Sarah Petronio, born to a musical family in Bombay, India, studied in New York with Henry LeTang before moving to Paris and encountering Jimmy Slyde, who became her mentor and dance partner. In 1993, she produced one of Chicago's first jazz tap festivals, Chicago On Tap, inviting teachers like Chuck Green, Jimmy Slyde, Acia Gray and Savion Glover. Sarah has appeared at festivals and in concerts around the world and continues to perform and conduct master classes and workshops. Still living in Paris, she is known for her fusions of live jazz music and tap dance and for her decidedly individual, feminine style.

Leela Petronio is a French-American teacher, choreographer and producer currently living in Paris. She studied with tap masters Sarah Petronio, Jimmy Slyde and Steve Condos, and has taught and performed around the world. Leela has danced for many years with the European cast of *Stomp* and is the artistic director for the Hip Tap Project, a percussive dance troupe that blends rhythm tap with hip hop, body percussion and live music.

Bill "Bojangles" Robinson (1878–1949), known for his precise, clear tap style, was considered one of the world's greatest dancers. He worked the vaudeville circuit until age fifty, then appeared to great acclaim in Lew Leslie's *The Blackbirds of 1928*, the first of six Broadway shows for Robinson. He soon became the highest-paid black performer in Hollywood history and was in great demand. He tapped in fourteen films with Shirley Temple; theirs was the first interracial dance team in Hollywood. When he died in 1949, more than half a million people lined the streets of New York for his funeral procession.

LaVaughn Robinson (1927–2008) was raised and trained on the streets of Philadelphia, where he was mentored by other great tappers such as Honi Coles, the Nicholas Brothers and the Condos Brothers. He performed on the big band circuit in the 1940s and '50s alongside his partner, Henry Meadows, but his best-known dance partner is Germaine Ingram, a former student. He later became a popular instructor around the country and held an appointment at Philadelphia's University of the Arts. Germaine continued to help him pass on the traditions of vernacular tap dance.

Sue Ronson (1931–2006) was a Boston-based teacher and choreographer who began her career at age four, dancing on Broadway alongside Ethel Merman in *Annie Get Your Gun*. She went on to perform with such legends as Frank Sinatra, Sammy Davis, Jr., Bob Hope and Burl Ives before joining the staff of the Boston Conservatory, where she taught for 22 years, propelling many of her students to Broadway and other stages nationwide.

Jason Samuels Smith, known for his speedy, intricate, and hard-hitting footwork, is an Emmy Award-winning teacher and choreographer based in New York City. The son of renowned jazz dancers JoJo Smith and Sue Samuels, he has toured with his own company, A.C.G.I. (Anybody Can Get It); *Chasin' the Bird: A Tribute to Charlie Parker*; and *India Jazz Suites*, a collaboration with Kathak dancer Pandit Chitresh Das. Jason was a principal cast member of the Broadway sensation *Bring In 'Da Noise, Bring In 'Da Funk*, as well as *Imagine Tap!*, and was featured in the short film *Tap Heat*.

Billy Siegenfeld is an Emmy Award-winning choreographer and performer and the Artistic Director of Jump Rhythm Jazz Project, a Chicago-based tap and jazz dance company. He is the creator of Jump Rhythm Technique®, a full-bodied, rhythm-first approach to dance theater. Billy is also a Charles Deering McCormick Professor of Teaching Excellence at Northwestern University. Visit jrjp.org for more information about the Jump Rhythm Technique®.

Jimmy Slyde (1927–2008), born James Godbolt, grew up in Massachusetts, where he met Jimmy "Sir Slyde" Mitchell, with whom he performed around the New England Big Band circuit as the Slyde Brothers. In the 1970s, he moved to Paris, where he introduced rhythm tap alongside Sarah Petronio and appeared in the jazz tap revue *Black and Blue*, which eventually went to Broadway. Jimmy Slyde also appeared in films, including *Tap*, and won several awards, including National Heritage and Guggenheim fellowships. Among tap dancers, he is often remembered as the "King of Slides" for his effortless slide technique.

Linda Sohl-Ellison is the cofounder, artistic director and choreographer of Rhapsody in Taps, a California-based performance company. She trained extensively with Foster Johnson, Eddie Brown, Honi Coles and Buster Brown, and collaborated with Gregory Hines. An award-winning artist, she appeared in the movie *Tap* as well as the documentaries *Thinking on Their Feet: Women of the Tap Renaissance*, *You Gotta Move* and *JUBA*. Linda has been a Professor of Dance at Orange Coast College in California since 1978.

Fred Strickler was cofounder and artistic director of the touring company Jazz Tap Ensemble and former dancer and choreographer with Rhapsody in Taps. A California-based performer, teacher and choreographer who has worked around the world, he has performed his "Tap Dance Concerto" with more than 40 orchestras. Fred has choreographed countless tap, modern and ballet works and taught for many years at University of California, Riverside. Beginning in 2010, he created and produced for YouTube "Masters of American Tap Dance," a series of ten-minute lessons with 37 master tap teachers.

Dormeshia Sumbry-Edwards, one of the leading female tap soloists and choreographers, known for her impeccable footwork and musicality, was featured on Broadway in *Black and Blue* and *Bring In 'Da Noise, Bring In 'Da Funk*. Also appearing in *Imagine Tap!* and the film *TAP*, she was private tap coach to Michael Jackson for over a decade. With tap-dancer husband Omar Edwards, Dormeshia runs the Harlem Tap Studio in New York City while teaching and performing around the world.

Aaron Tolson, best known for his six-year stint with *Riverdance*, is a New Hampshire-born, New York City-based teacher, performer, and choreographer. From 2006 to 2012, he directed and choreographed for his own company, the New England Tap Ensemble, which included children, teens and adults from around the region. With Derick Grant, he was co-creator, assistant choreographer and producer of *Imagine Tap!* and currently produces Tap2You, a national tap competition. Aaron is also a national spokesman for So-Danca tap shoes and founder and director of a new pre-professional tap company, Speaking in Taps.

Tony Waag is perhaps best known as the founder (in 2001) and director of Tap City: The New York City Tap Festival and the cofounder (in 1986) of the American Tap Dance Orchestra (now the American Tap Dance Foundation). He danced in the ATDO under the mentorship of Brenda Bufalino, with whom he cofounded Woodpeckers Tap Dance Center in New York City in 1989. Through the ATDF, Tony continues to produce regular performances, workshops, master classes, festivals, tap jams, student showcases and other tap events throughout New York City and around the world. He also operates the American Tap Dance Center, home of the ATDF, which features year-round tap classes for students of all ages.

Dianne Walker, affectionately called "Lady Di" within the tap community, is a master teacher based in Boston. A mentor to many tap dancers, particularly Savion Glover, she was an original cast member and later, assistant choreographer and dance captain of the show *Black and Blue*, a tap revue that arrived on Broadway in 1989 and featured Glover and tap masters Jimmy Slyde, Lon Chaney and Bunny Briggs. In her master classes, Dianne loves to tell stories and frequently shares material from her mentor, Leon Collins, with whom she studied alongside Barbara Duffy and Pamela Raff at his studio in Brookline, MA. Dianne also directed the inaugural tap program at the School at Jacob's Pillow and was the recipient of a *Dance Magazine* Lifetime Achievement Award in 2012.

Tap Legends to Know

HIGHLIGHTS OF TAP HISTORY

1600s   English people migrate to the United States, bringing social dance, waltzes, jigs, reels and clogs. At the same time, Africans come to America and bring percussive, grounded and syncopated rhythms.

1740   A law is passed forbidding slaves from playing drums or other instruments and from singing. Instead, they make music with clapping, body percussion, foot stomping and vocal intonations.

1825   The Erie Canal is completed, giving entertainers a new venue: showboats or "floating theaters."

1829   Thomas Rice develops the "Jump Jim Crow" dance, which mimics slaves' movements.

1840s   William Henry Lane, a free slave known as Juba, studies with an Irishman and does challenge matches with John Diamond, a white Irish minstrel dancer. Juba is later named the "king of all dancers" and becomes the only black man to perform with white minstrelsy. His influence is still seen in jazz and eccentric dance.

1845   The Irish potato famine forces many Irish people to migrate to America, bringing their jigs and reels. Those who settle in tenements share music with their African-American neighbors.

1845-   Minstrel shows, comedy, walk-around, variety acts and cakewalks become popular. New dance styles
1900   are developed: buck and wing, Irish jig, Virginia Essence, hornpipe, clogging, and soft shoe. Whites in blackface start imitating blacks.

1880s   Vaudeville establishes tap as an American art form. Black artists remain segregated from the white circuit. The Theatre Owners Booking Association (T.O.B.A.) is formed to book black artists.

Family-focused variety acts appear in theaters; they include acrobats, animal acts, legomania (rubber legs), toe tap, pedestal dance, sand dance, soft shoe and the buck and wing. Flash steps such as trenches, coffee grinds and Russian splits are developed.

Steps such as time steps and "falling off a log" become standardized and popular. Steps are also named after their cities of origin: Buffalo, Cincinnati, Charleston, and New Yorker. Other steps are named after dancers such as Maxie Ford, Bill Robinson break, Ruby Keeler time step.

Time steps set the tempo for the pianist. Early steps are named after the number of sounds following the hop: single, double or triple.

1910-   The Jazz Age brings Ragtime music, the Charleston, the Black Bottom and the Shimmy. Dance
1920s   marathons continue.

Men, women and families start performing groups such as Fred and Adele Astaire, the Cohans, the Seven Little Foys, the Five Kellys (with Gene Kelly), the Chorus Girls (the Tiller Girls) and the Condos Brothers. Leonard Reed creates the Shim-Sham Shimmy.

1915   Metal taps are added to tap shoes.

1920s   On the T.O.B.A. circuit, John Bubbles becomes known as "the father of rhythm tap." Peg Leg Bates, Baby Laurence, King Rastus Brown and others dance flat-footed in syncopated rhythm. There is a lot of improvisation and experimentation. Dancers are also musicians and conduct challenges with other dancers. Their style is close to the floor.

At the Hoofer's Club, on 131 St. and 7th Ave. in NYC, they say, "Thou shall not copy another's steps … exactly." Class acts develop, in which a duet or trio wears full evening attire. Suave, smooth Honi Coles and Cholly Atkins help to change jazz's image to one of sophistication.

1920-1933	During the time of Prohibition, the Cotton Club in Harlem is rocking!
1927	*The Blackbirds of 1928* is produced, starring Bill "Bojangles" Robinson. He performs on the balls of his feet, stands erect, and does the stair dance. He is also the first black star on Broadway and in an inter-racial team with Shirley Temple in films. During the Depression, the "talkies" end vaudeville. Many dancers, including Honi Coles and Cholly Atkins, emigrate to Europe. Others become teachers and choreographers, or go into film.
1930	Swing music and the Big Band era get people back on their feet, dancing to Benny Goodman, Duke Ellington, Count Basie and the Dorsey Brothers at places like the Savoy Ballroom. In Harlem, people do the lindy and the jitterbug. Swing music emphasizes a simple melody that allows for improvisation.
1930s-1950s	This is the era of dance movies starring Fred Astaire, Ginger Rogers, Eleanor Powell, Bill Robinson, Buddy Ebsen, James Cagney, Gene Kelly, Donald O'Connor, Gene Nelson, Ann Miller and others. These films blend ballroom and tap dancing and everyday life, with dancers in ordinary places. The movie *Singin' in the Rain*, starring Gene Kelly and Cyd Charisse, is released in 1952. The Nicholas Brothers are considered the "flash" artists of the 1930s with their hit *Stormy Weather*.
1940s	People enjoy the Big Bands in big ballrooms. Honi Coles appears with Cab Calloway, Baby Laurence with Duke Ellington, the Condos Brothers with Benny Goodman. Dancers improvise with the band, using counter rhythms. Tap dancers are considered part of the percussion section. Broadway shows feature choreographers and directors such as Agnes DeMille, Bob Fosse, Jerome Robbins, Gower Champion. Jazz and modern dance start taking the place of tap on stage.
1945-1950s	After WWII, people stay home more, listen to the radio or watch television. The jazz-dance scene develops with Matt Mattox, Luigi and Gus Giordano. Jazz dance and music become more recognized as individual, professional forms. There is a decline in big bands, but small combos become popular. People listen to jazz more than they dance, and less tap is heard on Broadway. In Boston, the Stanley Brown Studio opens.
1950s	Rock and Roll arrives with Elvis Presley, and people begin dancing "to" the music instead of "with" it. The jazz scene features the bebop music of Charlie Parker and Dizzy Gillespie in small clubs. Tap continues in small studios and clubs. It is a time of innovation and change. Classical tap is developed by Paul Draper and Danny Daniels. Morton Gould writes the popular "Tap Dance Concerto." The Copasetics are formed, including dancers Buster Brown, Ernest Brown, Leslie "Bubba" Gaines, Charles "Cookie" Cook and Honi Coles. They are "a benevolent organization dedicated to the memory of Mr. Robinson, who always said, 'Everything's copasetic.'" Small dance studios arise. Henry LeTang, Danny Hoctor, Charles Hughes, Charles Kelley and others open NYC dance complexes and private studios, providing instruction for all forms of dance. Eventually, rent increases and demolition force teachers to move out of the big dance clusters.
1960s	Music goes freestyle, with jazz creativity taking the lead. Tap is edged out by popular dances like the Twist, Frug, Pony and others. Marshall Stearns invites tap performers such as Honi Coles, Pete Nugent, Baby Laurence and Chuck Green to the Newport Jazz Festival. "Tap Happening" showcase with Leticia Jay leads to the formation of the *The Hoofers*, which opens at the Mercury Theater in 1969. The Duke Ellington band plays with Bunny Briggs as its solo performer in a sacred jazz concert.
1970s	Broadway revivals such as *No, No, Nanette* and movie reruns attract new tap students. Dance studios and colleges start teaching tap as well.

1979   Rap music enters the realm of commercial pop music, and hip hop dance becomes popular.

1980s   Jane Goldberg produces *By Word of Foot*, the first international tap festival at the New York City Village Gate.

Gregory Hines arrives on the scene in the movies *Tap and White Nights*, and on Broadway in *Jelly's Last Jam*. He introduces hoofers to a population that has never seen the masters perform live.

Tap companies are formed, and appear in concert halls. *The Tap Dance Kid*, *My One and Only* and *Crazy for You* become popular Broadway shows. Savion Glover takes over the title role of *The Tap Dance Kid* in 1984.

In 1986, Brenda Bufalino starts the American Tap Dance Orchestra, Heather Cornell founds Manhattan Tap; both NYC-based companies perform concert tap choreography. Lynn Dally starts Jazz Tap Ensemble on the West Coast.

1989   Congress establishes National Tap Dance Day to honor Bill "Bojangles" Robinson's birthday, May 25. The Colorado Dance Festival hosts a tap summit, inviting ambitious young tappers by audition to study intensively with master teachers like Steve Condos, Honi Coles and Buster Brown. Woodpeckers Dance Studio opens under the direction of Brenda Bufalino and Tony Waag.

1990s   Tap dance shows such as *Riverdance, Lord of the Dance, Stomp,* and *Tap Dogs* become popular worldwide. There is a resurgence of Irish step dancing in studios across the country. The roots of American tap dancing become more defined.

Savion Glover produces Emmy Award-winning *Bring In 'Da Noise, Bring In 'Da Funk* and makes regular appearances on PBS' *Sesame Street*. His broad exposure influences young people to tap to their own music, adding complex rhythms and improvisational, articulate footwork.

Lane Alexander cofounds the Chicago Human Rhythm Project, one of the nation's largest and best-known tap festivals, in 1990.

2000s   Tony Waag, founds Tap City: The New York City Tap Festival, in 2001. In 2002, the ATDO is renamed the American Tap Dance Foundation. *Imagine Tap!*, the first full-length rhythm-tap revue since *Noise/ Funk*, runs for several weeks at Chicago's Harris Theater. Created and choreographed by Derick Grant and Aaron Tolson, the show features popular tappers such as Michelle Dorrance, Ayodele Casel, Jason Samuels Smith, Chloe Arnold, Dormeshia Sumbry-Edwards and Ray Hesselink, along with live music and hip hop dancers. Many veteran hoofers, including Buster Brown, the Nicholas Brothers, Jimmy Slyde and LaVaughn Robinson, pass away, significantly diminishing that generation of tap dancers.

2010s   In 2010, the School at Jacob's Pillow hosts its inaugural tap program, curated by Dianne Walker. The American Tap Dance Foundation gains a permanent home in NYC's Greenwich Village, where it continues to offer year-round tap classes, residencies, workshops and performance opportunities for all ages, as well as affordable rehearsal space. Michelle Dorrance, whom the New York Times declares a "talented choreographer, the most promising one in tap right now," premieres a company, Dorrance Dance, at NYC's Danspace in 2011. She receives a 2011 Bessie Award, a 2012 Princess Grace Award and a 2013 Jacob's Pillow Award for her innovative work, becoming one of tap's most popular choreographers. The Kennedy Center presents its first full-length tap concert, in tandem with the Chicago Human Rhythm Project, in 2012; it features a variety of master tap dancers and youth companies. Tap festivals continue to flourish nationally and internationally, offering more and more dancers the opportunity to study and perform with master teachers.

RESOURCES

Bufalino, Brenda. *Tapping the Source: Tap Dance Stories, Theory and Practice*. Codhill Press, 2004.

Fletcher, Beverly. *Tapwork*. Beverly Fletcher, 1997.

Frank, Rusty E. *Tap*. William Morrow and Company, 1990.

Goldberg, Jane. *Shoot Me While I'm Happy*. Changing Times Tap Dancing Co., 2008.

Gudat, Diane. *Time Step Dictionary*. Self-published, dianegudat.wordpress.com.

Hill, Constance Vallis. *Tap Dancing America: A Cultural History*. Oxford University Press, 2010.

Stearns, Marshall and Jean. *Jazz Dance: The Story of American Vernacular Dance*. DaCapo Press, 1994; Schirmer Books, 1968.

Recommended reading for young children to open discussion about tap dance:

Ackerman, Karen. *Song and Dance Man*. Dragonfly Books, Alfred A. Knopf, 1988.

Glover, Savion and Bruce Weber. *My Life in Tap*. William Morrow and Company, 2000.

Haver, Nancy. *What Tap Dancing's All About: According to Dr. Jeni LeGon*. Warbler Press, 2005.

Michelson, Richard. *Happy Feet: The Savoy Ballroom Lindy Hoppers and Me*. Gulliver Books, Harcourt, 2005.

Osborne, M.D. *The Boy Who Loved to Shim-Sham Shimmy*. Wooden Shoe Press, 2004.

Recommended videos to bring tap choreography and history alive:

By Word of Foot: Tap Masters Pass on Their Traditions. Produced by Jane Goldberg. Changing Times Tap, 1980. Included with purchase of Jane Goldberg's book, *Shoot Me While I'm Happy* (Changing Times Tap Dancing Co., 2008), if purchased from: janegoldberg.org/book.html.

Gene Kelly: Anatomy of a Dancer. Directed by Robert Trachtenberg. Warner Home Video, 2002. DVD available through Amazon and other sites.

Great Feats of Feet: A Portrait of the Jazz and Tap Dancer. American Tap Dance Foundation, 1977. DVD available for purchase at: atdf.org/shop/DVDsInfo.html.

Honi Coles: The Class Act of Tap. Produced by Susan Pollard. Directed by Jim Swenson. AcinemaApart.com. DVD available for purchase at: justtap.com/master/jtmedia.asp.

Josh Hilberman Presents Cappella Josh; *Josh Hilberman Presents Passin' The Buck & Wing*; *Josh Hilberman Presents Rhythm Tap Dance Time Steps.* DVDs available for purchase at: hilbermania.com.

Someone Stole the Baby: A Documentary on Brenda Bufalino and the American Tap Dance Orchestra. American Tap Dance Foundation, 1991. DVD available for purchase at: atdf.org/shop/DVDsInfo.html.

Steve Condos' Tap Dance Workout DVD. Produced by Steve Condos, Lorraine Condos and Mark Weissbert.

Tap. Starring Gregory Hines et al. Directed by Nick Castle. Sony Pictures Home Entertainment, 2006. DVD available through Amazon and other sites.

PHOTO CREDITS

GLOSSARY

AST	at same time
ATF	across the floor
BC	ball change
br	brush
coupé	a ballet term used to indicate a placement of one foot turned out in front of the other
CRRL	cramp roll
fl	flap
gr	grab off
hdig	heel dig
hdrp	heel drop
hstand	heel stand
L	left
pb	pull back
pu	pick up
R	right
sc	scuff
sh	shuffle
sl	slap
sp	spank
st	step
STA	stamp
STO	stomp
tdig	toe dig
tdrp	toe drop
tip	toe tip

Stage Directions

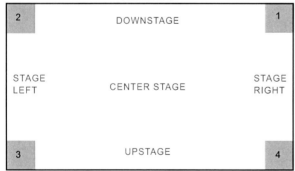

Additional Notes about Classic Tap Steps and Phrases

Back and Front Essence - a common idea in soft-shoe dancing, the essences cross front or back in a series of steps and ball changes and can be done single or double.

Bombershay - a traveling step that uses a step, spank, step and is often used in traditional buck-and-wing and Broadway choreography. The second step is sometimes a heel dig.

Buffalo - commonly called "Shuffle off to Buffalo," this step was made popular in the late 19th century by the showman Pat Rooney. It travels with a leap, shuffle, leap.

188

Call and Response - in tap dance, a succession of two distinct phrases usually played by different dancers, where the second phrase is heard as a direct commentary on or response to the first.

Canon - a musical form in which dancers, individually or in groups, begin one after another at regular intervals successively taking up the same phrase.

Cincinnati - history suggests that this combination of a spank, heel drop and shuffle step originated in Cincinnatti in the 1950s.

Condos Rudiments - small footwork exercises developed by Steve Condos to increase speed and clarity.

Cramp Rolls - a classic combination of steps and heel drops, commonly done in a RLRL pattern. A "roll" is often associated with a step and heel drop.

Drawbacks - usually associated with a three-sound phrase that includes a step, spank and heel drop and that travels back.

Grapevine - a vine-like movement with the feet alternately crossing back and front.

Irish - a common step in Irish Step Dancing, consisting of a shuffle, hop, step.

Maxie Ford - created by and named for the vaudevillian Maxie Ford, the step consists of a step (or leap), shuffle, leap, tip.

Paddle and Roll - sometimes called a paradiddle or "the Hollywood roll." Dancers such as John Bubbles and Steve Condos, both famous for their rhythmic dance creations, popularized it.

Paddle Turn - a step commonly used in soft shoe that begins with a step or flap with ball changes that move around the perimeter.

Scissors Step - commonly used in soft shoe, a step that resembles a scissors, in which the feet cross with a ball change and open with a leap, heel dig, and then cross and open again.

Shim Sham (Shim-Sham Shimmy) - a 32-bar dance performed by tap dancers around the world, often at the end of a program. Often attributed to Leonard Reed, who originally called it Goofus, or to Willie Bryant, it has also been credited to chorus-line dancers. It is a "national anthem" of swing dancers.

Soft Shoe - a style of dancing done in soft shoes, dating back to the 1920s.

Sugarfoot - a twisting movement popular in vernacular style dance.

Tack Annie (Tacky Annie) - the third step of the Shim-Sham Shimmy; many historians claim it was named after a woman named Annie who ran a bar.

Time Steps - a pattern of steps, usually reversed every 4 counts, that originally were used by vaudevillians to help set the tempo for musicians.

Varsity Drag - a dance originated in 1927 in the play *Good News*, often accompanied by arms pushing up and down.

Waltz Clog - a step that dates back to clogging's earliest roots. Done in 3/4 time, it consists of a step, shuffle, ball change.

SAMPLE LESSON PLAN

WEEK 5   LEVEL III   MINUTES 45

Min.	Skills and Series Development
6	Rudiments – "Peanut" p. 96 Stationary - Review #1–4, introduce #5 (8th notes) p. 96 Traveling - Review #1–6, introduce #7 (8th notes)
10	Double Heels – "Oobabaloo" p. 138 Press cramp rolls - Review #1–4, swing with half-turn p. 139 Cramp rolls - Review #1–4, teach exercise #5
6	Shuffles – "'A,' You're Adorable" p. 111 #5, a.–j. with crossing and uncrossing
3	Slaps and Flaps – "Jeepers Creepers" p. 124 Begin flap progressions
15	Center Floor – "MacNamara's Band" p. 41 BC combo, a. b. c. d. Go through entire series
	Across the Floor
	Combo/Choreography
5	Tap Fun – Improvisation Call and response

 **TAP NOTES**

LESSON PLAN

DATE / WEEK _____ LEVEL ___1___ MINUTES _____

Min.	Skills and Series Development
	Rudiments
	Marches
	Shuffles
	Across the Floor
	Center Floor
	Combo/Choreography
	Tap Fun

 **TAP NOTES**

LESSON PLAN

DATE / WEEK _____ LEVEL _2 & 3_ MINUTES _____

Min.	Skills and Series Development
	Rudiments
	Double Heels
	Ball Changes
	Shuffles
	Slaps and Flaps
	Across the Floor
	Center Floor
	Combo/Choreography
	Tap Fun

LESSON PLAN

DATE / WEEK _____ LEVEL _4 & 5_ MINUTES_____

Min.	Skills and Series Development
	Rudiments
	Double Heels
	Shuffles
	Spanks
	Paddle and Roll
	Slaps and Flaps
	Across the Floor
	Center Floor/Combo/Choreography
	Tap Fun

22670028R00111

Made in the USA
San Bernardino, CA
16 July 2015